AF408616

From the 'Dismal Science' to The Economics of Jubilation through Concordian economics

Carmine Gorga

CIP a Camerei Naționale a Cărții

Gorga, Carmine

From the "Dismal Science" to The Economics of Jubilation through : Concordian economics / Carmine Gorga. – Chişinău : Generis Publishing, 2020 (Print on demand). – 165 p. : fig., tab.

Referinţe bibliogr. la sfârşitul cap.

ISBN 978-9975-3421-6-2.

330.1

G 70

Cover Image: Wikimedia Commons, Michelangelo's Moses, San Pietro in Vincoli(Rome)

Online orders: www.generis-publishing.com
Orders by email: info@generis-publishing.com

Books by the Author

Jubilee 2020, Generis Publishing, 2020

The Redemption of the Bully: Through Love, Toward the Beloved Community. Scholars' Press, 2018.

The Economic Process: An Instantaneous Non-Newtonian Picture Third Edition, The Somist Institute, 2016.

The Centrality of the Resurrection: Are We Ready to Let Jesus Enter our Hearts? (Relationalism) (Volume 2), The Somist Institute, 2016.

A Case for God: In Search of a Humanism Filled with True Human Beings, (Relationalism) (Volume 1), The Somist Institute, 2014.

The Economic Process: An Instantaneous Non-Newtonian Picture. Lanham, Md. and Oxford: University Press of America, 2009, expanded softcover edition.

To My Polis, With Love: May Gloucester Show the World the Ways of Frugality, The Somist Institute, 2008.

To My Polis, With Love: May Gloucester Show the World the Ways of Frugality, The Somist Institute, 2008, Kindle edition.

The Economic Process: An Instantaneous Non-Newtonian Picture. Lanham, Md. and Oxford: University Press of America, 2002.

Quality Assurance of Seafood (with Louis J. Ronsivalli), Van Nostrand Reinhold, 1988, hardcover.

You have written a truly monumental paper... Only one very, very small minor point separates us. I feel your criticism of Adam Smith is too harsh....

Prof. Michael E. Brady

I finally got a chance to read your text and it is indeed an incredibly original treatment of the whole issue. I have to read it again to understand some of the economic points, but the overall historical and moral treatment was immediately within the layman's reach and very impressive. Congratulations!

Prof. John C. Rao

Thank you for your stimulating paper. It is evidently full of stimulating and valuable ideas. Since I have not done any work on these matters, there is nothing I can add aside from my best wishes.

Prof. William J. Baumol

Have you taught? I think you have; you teach the reader, or make the reader pause and reflect on how beautifully simple life could be.

Teresa Arnold

The paper on Keynes is brilliant.

Prof. John C. Médaille

I=C, I love it! In fact, I think Keynes's General Theory is incoherent without it... Someday, I=C will shift from radically ridiculous to patently obvious. I hope you get some of the credit.

A correspondent who wishes to remain anonymous

Expanded third edition (of *The Economic Process*) presents the transformation of economic theory into Concordian economics, shifting the understanding of the economic system from a mechanical, Newtonian entity to a more dynamic, relational process.

Journal of Economic Literature

<h1 align="center">Acknowledgments/History</h1>

This book is a compilation of essays published over the decades. Chapter 1 is a reduced version of my presentation to the Gloucester Writers Center on March 4, 2020. It is designed as a fast introduction to the main topic, namely the transformation of the "dismal science" of economics to The Economics of Jubilation—through Concordian economics.

Chapter 2 is titled "A Revision of Keynes' Model." It started from a summer of intense intellectual struggle with the General Theory in 1965, in which I squeezed all the excess verbiage from the word Saving and reduced it to Hoarding. This chapter was written in July 1974, reformatted with a subtitle, an abstract, a prescript, and a bio added in June 2008. It was posted on SSRN on August 22, 2009.

Chapter 3 is titled "Concordian economics: An Overall View." It was published by *Econintersect* on January 2, 2017. Econintersect is among the Top 100 Sites for Enlightened Economists.

Chapter 4 is titled "Concordian economics: On the transformation of the "dismal science of economics into The Economics of Jubilation." This paper was presented at the IPSI Conference in Amalfi on March 5, 2010 for *Transactions on Advanced Research*, and posted at https://papers.ssrn.com/sol3/papers.cfm?abstract_id=1600919, 6 May 2010.

Chapter 5 is titled "Economics of Jubilation - Blinking Adam's Fallacy Away." This work was originally published in Albert Tavidze, ed., *Progress in Economics Research*, Vol. 19. Hauppauge, NY: Nova Science Publishers, 2011, pp, 1-40.

Chapter 6 is titled "The Lender Is Not a Hoarder." It was originally published by *Econintersect* on January 28,2020.

Chapter 7 is titled "Cancel Student Debt? NO!! Cancel ALL Debt." It was published by *Econintersect* on January 28, 2020.

Chapter 8 is titled "Two Proposals to Stabilize the Monetary System." It is a compilation of four papers published by *Mother Pelican – A Journal of Solidarity and Sustainability* respectively in September, October, December 2015 and January 2016.

Chapter 9 is titled "We Must Redirect Our National Credit." It was published by *TalkMarkets* on March 17, 2020.

TO ALL
SINCEREST THANKS

Carmine Gorga

Gloucester, MA
March 19, 2020

Table of Contents

Introduction

This book is a brief introduction to our 4,000 years history of economic thought. The story starts with Adam Smith. He did a few things: he expunged morality from the social sciences; he obliterated the word Hoarding from the economic language; and he destroyed the long history of economic justice from our collective memory. (For a full assessment, one must put him within the "spirit of the time"; also, one must separate his thought from such successors' actions and thought as Jeremy Bentham.)

What has Adam Smith wrought? One revolution after another, and, lately, as widely acknowledged, a condition of crisis in economic theory. The faults of economic practice today are unspeakable.

To resolve the current crisis in economic theory we must reacquire an understanding of the phenomenon of Hoarding. This phenomenon pops up in our consciousness as soon as we select one definition out of the 100,000 possible definitions of Saving that, following Adam Smith, exist in mainstream economic theory today. Once we discover that Saving cannot mean other than passive, nonproductive wealth, we become entitled to jettison the word Saving and replace it with the word Hoarding.

The word Hoarding allows us to rediscover a group of Jubilees proclaimed by Moses. In this work we will place special attention to the Seven Year Jubilee concerning the cancellation of debts. We thus become emboldened enough to call, not only for the cancellation of student debts, but for the *systematic* cancellation of all debt every seven years.

If we succeed in doing that, we might not only unburden mankind of tremendous loads on the shoulder of most human beings; we might even be able to resolve the current catastrophic financial crisis—with little or no damage to anyone. We will defuse the bomb of the ongoing Wall Street crash.

Whether or not we are able to solve the many problems generated by uncollectable debt, we might soon direct our gaze to the methods used by our Central Banks to create and distribute money. From a mysterious activity, the process of creating and distributing new money will be seen as a simple, productive, and just chain of decisions that will shift our national credit—our "money," our commonwealth—from Wall Street to Main Street. If this policy is implemented at the earliest possible moment, the damage to the real economy caused by the Wall Street crash will be either null or enormously mitigated.

Through these ancient-novel solutions of the economic problem finally put in place, we will gradually grant us all a prize that we have so painfully forever been looking for, economic freedom achieved through economic *justice* for all. And I mean conjoined with economic freedom for all. The affluent can keep all the wealth they have accumulated so far; there is no need for re-distribution of wealth. There is only the need for a fair distribution of ownership as wealth is being created.

Going back from Adam Smith to Moses is facilitated by Concordian economics. Concordian economics evolves, naturally and organically, from the definition of Hoarding. Once we put Hoarding in relation to all other major concepts/factors of economic theory and practice, we discover the definition of Investment, a definition that is still nonexistent in mainstream economics. Investment is Income minus Hoarding. We really have no choice about "consumption" of wealth, if we want to stay alive. The real choice is between Hoarding and Investing one's talents, one's financial as well as spiritual talents.

A chain of mathematical/logical reasoning yields the equivalence of Production to Distribution to Consumption. This relation is the essence of the economic process. Even when we purchase a chocolate bar we get engaged in one small cycle of the economic process: We exchange money for real wealth, and we safely get out of the store because we carry with us a sales slip. This is legal proof of proper ownership of the chocolate bar.

We really do not need to learn much more about economic theory. A couple of observations: Professor Michael E. Brady, reviewing my fundamental book titled *The Economic Process,* highlighted the central core of that book, namely the function of Hoarding. He stated:

Gorga's (G) concern is to identify what the fundamental problem is that prevents such a system from obtaining AND MAINTAINING a full employment level of output. Why is such an economy subject to a destabilizing boom-bust business cycle over time? G is one of the very few economists to identify the fundamental problem as hoarding behavior. Hoarding means that the individual is not spending his income on consumption goods, investment goods, public goods, exported goods or imported goods. Hoarding problems will manifest themselves at the macroscopic level. Thus, involuntary unemployment can be identified as a macro problem that results from the microscopic hoarding behaviors of many individuals but will not be susceptible to a purely micro analysis based on utility maximization subject to an income constraint problem. It is an effective demand problem that shows up at the aggregate level. This, naturally, may present a major stumbling block for a modern day economist who believes that all macro behavior is merely the sum of all micro behavior.

G also shows that this is the major problem that has impacted all types of economies over the last 4,000 years and not just capitalist economies. This is also the major economic problem that has been identified by the Roman Catholic church during the many centuries that humans were subject to great uncertainty. Technically, it is impossible to eliminate all uncertainty which means that hoarding will be a problem. However, once identified, it's negative impact can be reduced to a minimum. Keynes states this on pp.241-42 and 351-52 but does not emphasize it for his economist audience. G emphasizes it and convincingly identifies it as the main problem.

Yes. Once we plot the Hoarding/Investment relationship on a graph, we clearly see that more hoarding, less growth; more hoarding, more inflation; more hoarding more poverty.

It took Vincent Ferrini, our first Gloucester Poet Laureate, to identify the essence of Concordian economics. Reviewing the same book for our local paper, he stated: "(Concordian economics) has the answers to universal poverty and the anxieties of the affluent."

Precisely. Concordian economics makes it clear that we do not need one cent, let alone two cents, of other people's money to set right the many wrongs that beset our modern world. We only need *economic* justice, the respect of peoples' economic rights, a feat that can be accomplished only through the practice of economic responsibilities. We then achieve the common good.

It took me forty years to realize that "Investment = Income – Hoarding" is nothing but the mathematical formulation of the Parable of the Talents. Naturally. What else to expect from Jesus?

Chapter 1: A PowerPoint Presentation

Images are worth a thousand words. The following slides offer us the opportunity to run through the whole argument of this book with the help of the following images. This is the argument:

1. The "dismal science" of economics is not a science:

2. Using the tools of supply and demand, economics—by general admission—runs into a "black box," from which it cannot scientifically determine the trend:

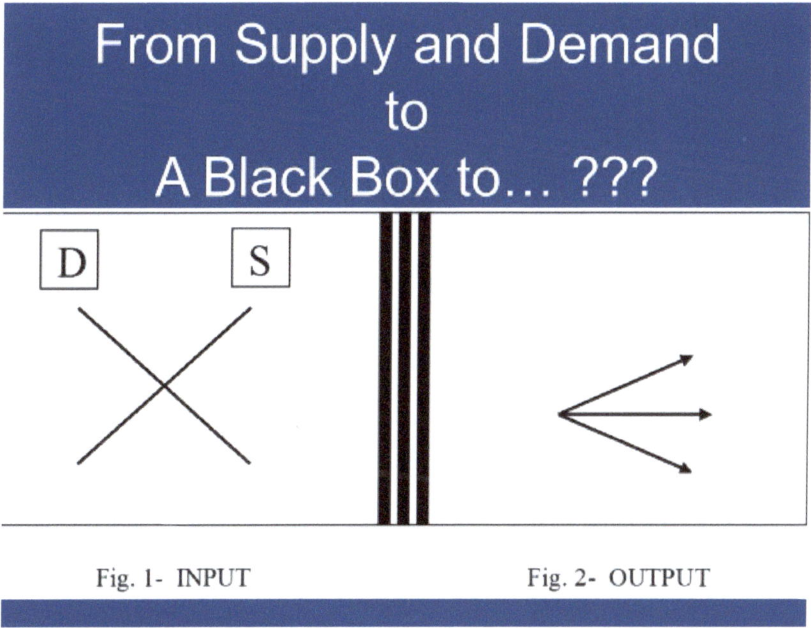

3. Concordian economics puts at its core the study of the economic process:

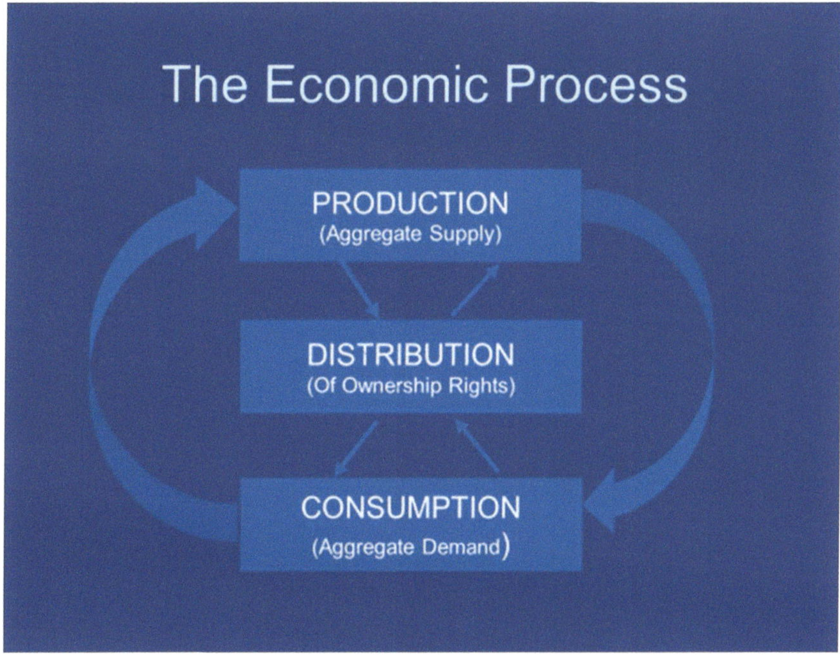

4.   The economic process is revealed by revising Keynes' model of the economic system, namely by reducing the vague idea of saving into hoarding:

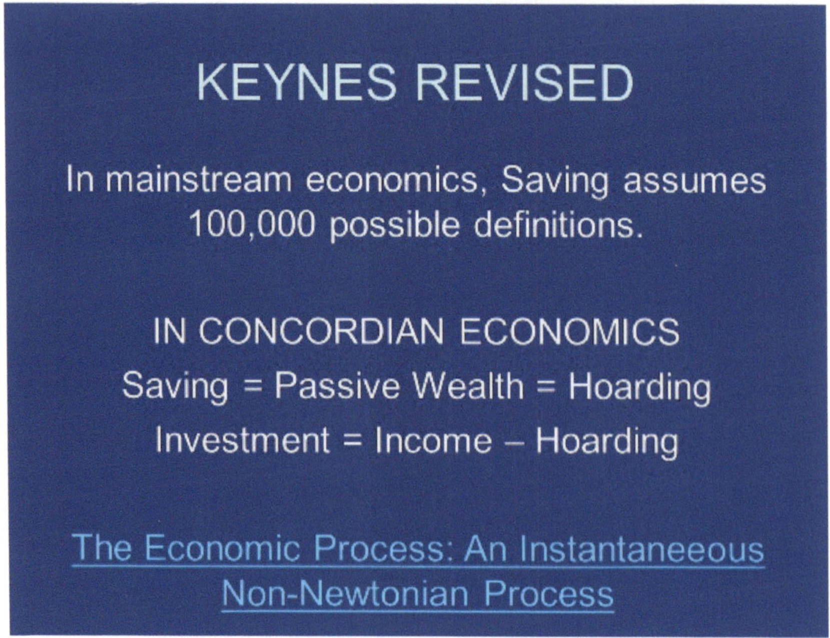

5.   The effects of hoarding are mostly self-evident. Its main benefit is that it brings us back to Moses:

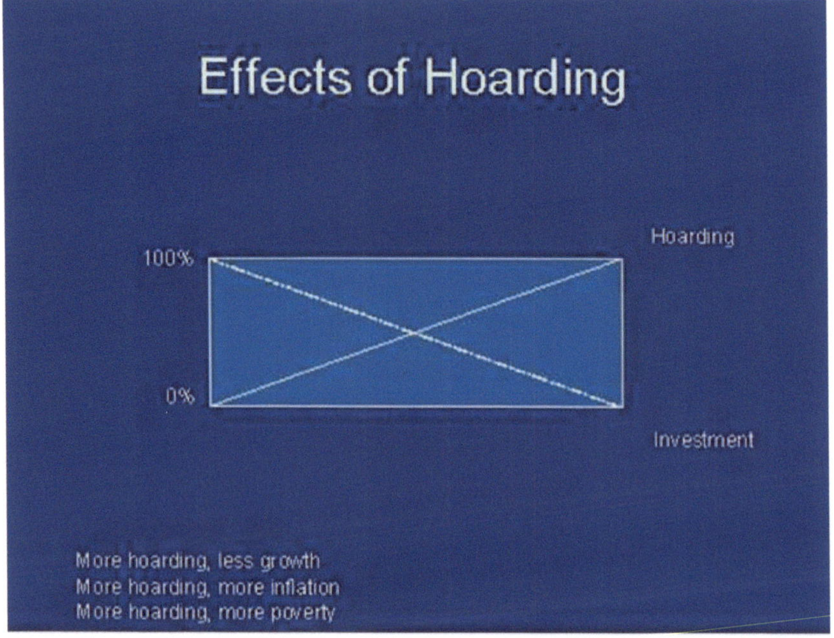

6.   Moses prescribed four forms of jubilee; we will concentrate on one of them: the cancellation of debts:

7. The wisdom of Moses is based on the revelation that, if debts are cancelled systematically, human relationships remain unaffected:

8.   How is money created? Would not hydraulic engineers direct the flow of funds straight to the people who need money?

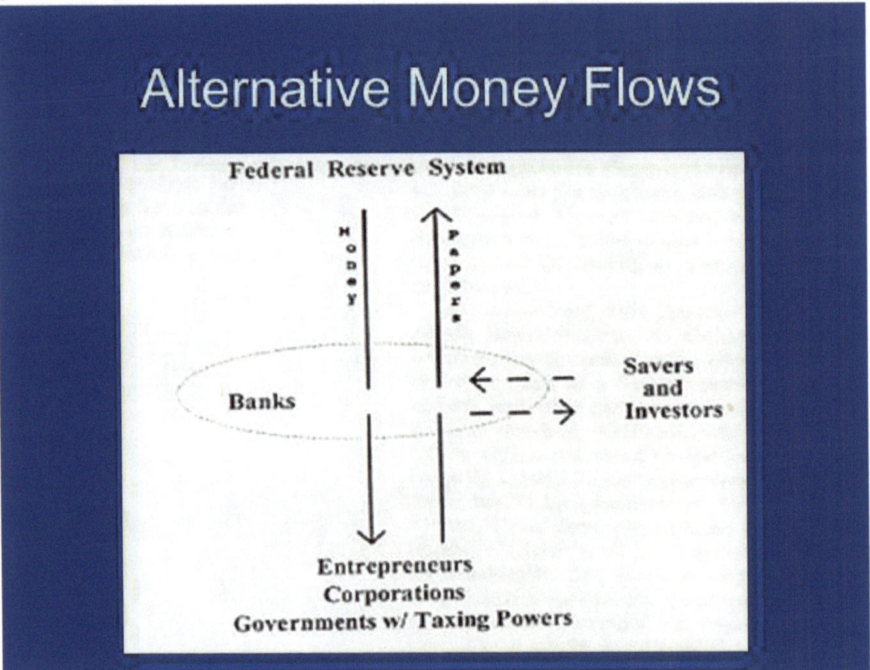

9.   It is recommended that money be created as loans, respecting three strict conditions:

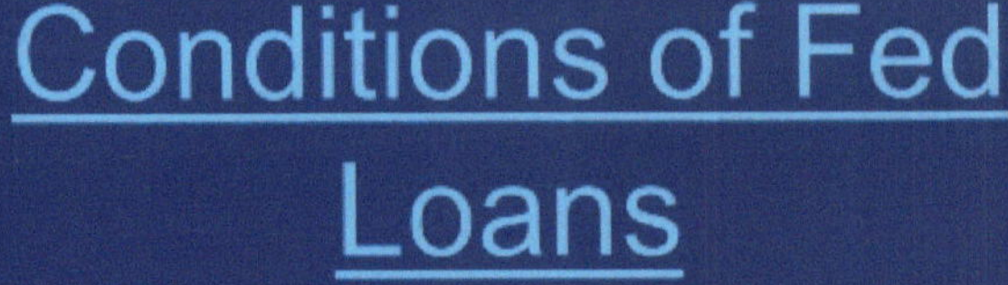

Chapter 2: A Revision of Keynes' Model

Abstract

This paper revises the "forms," not the substance, of Keynes' ideas. The first part of the paper analyzes weaknesses in Keynes' original model; the second part suggests remedies and, ultimately, a new model of the macrosystem; the third part provides an overview of the implications of the new model.

***

It is in the nature of things that the bold and elegant Keynesian synthesis should have given way to a generation of analysis. Recalling the closing sentences of the *General Theory*, we would indeed upset Keynes' calendar concerning the development of economic ideas were we not now to provide a new synthesis. An initial attempt toward this aim is presented in this paper.

The source from which we shall draw is, of course, the *General Theory*—a work which, very few have consistently denied, represents a marking stone in the development of economic thought. To acknowledge the significance of that work, however, should not prevent one from assessing its weaknesses. Indeed, as shall be seen, Keynes himself was fully aware of those weaknesses. They centered around the choice of the "forms" he adopted to express his ideas.

The first part of this paper shall analyze those weaknesses; the second part shall suggest remedies and, ultimately, a new model of the macrosystem; the third part shall provide an overview of the implications of the new model.

A few months after the *General Theory* was published, Keynes warned his early critics: "I am more attached to the comparatively simple fundamental ideas which underlie my theory than to the particular forms in which I have embodied them, and I have no desire that the latter should be crystallized at the present stage of the debate."[1] In the same article, as shall be seen later on, Keynes even changed those forms—and changed them along the lines suggested here. Yet, not too much weight has evidently been attached to his words; and not too much weight shall be attached to this argument in this paper. We shall rather try to heed that warning.

---

[1] Keynes, 1937a, p. 183.

The overall mold into which Keynes cast his thought is the well-known model:

$$Y = C + I$$
$$S = Y - C$$
$$S = I$$

where, Y = income; C = consumption; I = investment; S = saving.

Instead of analyzing how the model works (or it is presumed to work[2]), we shall step out of its internal logic and consistency and shall analyze the definitions of each one of its component parts. It is well in fact to remember that the validity of that model resides in pure logic. Or, enlarging the range of application of the following words by Abba Lerner: "It follows from and is implicit in our definitions of income, consumption, savings and investment, and the postulate that in any period moneys paid out are equal to moneys received."[3] Once those definitions are accepted, it is illogical to take issue with any of the implications inherent in that model. This is not the line of thought followed here. We shall rather isolate those definitions from the model and shall take issue with them directly.

We shall start with the analysis of the concept of saving. This concept is not formally defined in the *General Theory*. The most precise definition which, with the help of Leijonhufvud, one can reach is that of "non-consumption."[4] As Keynes was well aware, this is an "old-fashioned" definition.[5] It has a *formal* validity only in relation to its equality to investment. (A relationship which was powerfully reinforced by the formulation of Keynes' model.) Yet, substantially—as Keynes stressed—this definition of saving is "incomplete and misleading."[6]

It assumes that all *individual* savings are indeed investment; that they indeed represent a net addition to (or at least a replacement of) the *national* stock of investment. Instead, as Keynes repeatedly emphasized, savings can be simple *transfers* of wealth among individual persons.[7] Thus, that definition is incomplete. And it can also be misleading because it explains away what in the first decades of this century, especially through the inquiry of Robertson and Keynes, came to be

---

[2] *Cf.* Klein, esp. p. 83.

[3] Lerner, p. 625. The author was making exclusive reference to the equality of S to I.

[4] Leijonhufvud, pp. 28-29.

[5] *General Theory*, p. 83 and Keynes, 1937b, p. 249. To be precise, Keynes used the qualification "old-fashioned" for the entire proposition of the equality of S to I. The emphasis, however, was on the concept of saving.

[6] *General Theory*, p. 83.

[7] *Ibid.*, esp. pp. 83-85 and 212.

identified as the central economic problem: the "savings-investment nexus"; or, in different terms, how savings are transformed into investment; or, at a deeper level of analysis, the reasons for the fluctuations in the rate of investment.[8]

The merits of these issues are well-known and do not need to be restated. What is important to stress is: (a) that there are inherent weaknesses in the definition of saving used by Keynes, and (b) that Keynes was well aware of these weaknesses. A simple operation shall highlight this point. In mathematics, one of the conditions of equivalence is that the terms be symmetric.[9] If the equivalence of S to I, therefore, is valid, one should be able to substitute one of the terms with the other and obtain the same logical results. Substituting S with I in the first equation of Keynes' model, one obtains the following results:

$$Y = C + S$$
$$S = Y - C$$
$$S = S.$$

From this conclusion, it is impossible to reconstruct the equivalence of S to I without running into the error against which Keynes repeatedly warned:

> The error lies in proceeding to the plausible inference that, when an individual saves, he will increase aggregate investment by an equal amount. It is true, that, when an individual saves he increases his own wealth. But the conclusion that he also increases aggregate wealth fails to allow for the possibility that an act of individual saving may react on someone else's savings and hence on someone else's wealth.[10]

With two more statements, Keynes left little room for misunderstanding. First: "Every such attempt to save more by reducing consumption will so affect incomes that the attempt necessarily defeats itself."[11] Second: "This is the vital difference between the theory of the economic behaviour of the aggregate and the theory of the behaviour of the individual unit, in which we assume that changes in the individual's own demand do not affect his income."[12]

---

[8] *Ibid. Cf.* also Lekachman, pp. 67-73
[9] Suppes, pp. 213-220.
[10] *General Theory*, pp. 83-84. *Cf.* also pp. 177-178.
[11] *Ibid.*, p. 84.
[12] *Ibid.*, p. 85.

Without entering too deeply into the merit of the issues, it might be well to point out how—it is here believed—Keynes overcame the weaknesses in the definition of saving. In the *General Theory* and afterwards (but not in the *Treatise on Money*, obviously[13])—*when speaking of the equality of S to I,*—Keynes repeatedly refused to give any content to the concept of saving. While he provided a detailed list of the content of investment,[14] he steadfastly refused to provide any such list for the concept of saving. *Neither did he ever state that its content was identical to that of investment.* Rather, he used such similes as "bilateral character of the transactions between the producer on the one hand and, on the other, the consumer and purchaser of capital equipment";[15] or, "two-sided transaction" represented by the depositor's relation to his bank;[16] or, "there cannot be a buyer without a seller";[17] or, the law of demand and supply.[18] In other words, he consistently refused to give to the concept of saving its traditional content.

It seems clear, whenever he spoke of the equality of S to I, Keynes simply talked of saving *in terms of* investment—not the other way around. The difference is substantial. To every increase (or decrease) of investment, there must be an increase (or decrease) of assets; and these assets must necessarily be owned by somebody, they must correspond to someone's "savings."[19] Yet, every increase (or decrease) of saving will not correspond to an increase (or decrease) of investment. This device, together with his warning that the definition of saving he had accepted is "incomplete and misleading," left him free to analyze some of the concrete functions which saving—independent of investment—performs in the economic system.[20]

---

[13] *Treatise*, esp. Vol. I, pp. 123-126.

[14] *General Theory*, esp. pp. 74-75.

[15] *Ibid.*, p. 63.

[16] *Ibid.*, p. 81.

[17] *Ibid.*, p. 85.

[18] Keynes, 1937b, p. 249.

[19] This interpretation implies that the equilibrium between saving and investment is *instantaneous* and continuous. In the *General Theory*, pp. 183-184, Keynes in fact stressed that: "Saving and Investment are the determinates of the system, not the determinants. They are the twin results of the system's determinants, namely, the propensity to consume, the schedule of the marginal efficiency of capital and the rate of interest." (Italics added). *Cf.* also p. 328.
Consequently, this interpretation also implies that one cannot accept Keynes' classifications and admit a difference between ex-ante and ex-post saving (as Robertson is entitled to do), or between "observable savings" and "schedules of savings" (Klein, pp. 91-92 and 110-117), or between *actual* and *desired* savings (Hansen, p. 225), or any other such distinction.
On the other hand, it should not be denied that there are passages in the *General Theory* which—if read literally—might lead to a different interpretation than the one provided in the text. *Cf.*, esp. pp. 74, 117, 122-123, and Chapter 14.

[20] *General Theory*, esp. pp. 210-213.

Keynes then felt free to proceed with his analysis of the concept of investment—the analysis which he really meant to concentrate upon in the *General Theory*. Of concern here is neither this analysis nor the definition of investment—provided this concept is agreed to mean any addition to (or replacement of) the stock of productive wealth or all productive wealth per se. Of concern here are the implications of this concept.

The first obvious implication is that investment is assumed to be the motor of the economic system. This implication is so obvious and evidently so taken for granted that two of its ineluctable consequences are rarely taken into consideration: (1) if the abstract concept of investment is related to concrete human beings, it must be concluded that the motor of the economic system is the entrepreneur;[21] (2) if, as Keynes pointed out, Consumption—to repeat the obvious—is the sole end and object of all economic activity,"[22] it must be concluded that there is a minor contradiction in point of logic here: the dictates of deductive logic should compel one to start the analysis from the ultimate end—consumption—and not an intermediary one such as investment.

The second implication of the concept of investment is perhaps more serious. The equation $Y = C + I$ can be considered simultaneously with the equation $S = Y - C$ only if the entrepreneur—in his official capacity, not as a private individual—can ever be assumed to engage in the act of saving. Yet, in strict logic and outside of the validity of the equality of S to I, the entrepreneur cannot functionally save *and* invest—either at the same time or at successive periods. Retained earnings by a corporate enterprise clearly represent investment either imposed upon or allowed by the stockholders—and so are the retained earnings of an unincorporated enterprise. They represent income which, more or less consciously, is automatically reinvested. Retained earnings cannot represent savings, unless the meaning of this term is bent out of recognition to suit every purpose.

Those two equations cannot be made to refer to the consumer either, because otherwise the entrepreneur is eliminated from the field of observation. Even less tenable would be the proposition that the first equation refers to the entrepreneur and

---

[21] The relevance of this observation resides in the obvious linkage which exists between economics and the larger social and cultural context: *viz.*, the Protestant/Puritan ethic; *viz.*, the social and political status accorded to the businessman in the contemporary world.

[22] *General Theory*, p. 104.

the second to the consumer. Yet, these are the only alternatives warranted by that model; and none is entirely satisfactory.

The concept of consumption as used in Keynes' model also presents some difficulties. This concept has two meanings, yet only one of them—the negative one—is stressed in that model. (In contrast to the model, the General Theory stresses instead the second meaning.)

Etymologically, consumption means: (a) to take wholly or to destroy; (b) to spend. Destruction of wealth occurs only with obsolescence and natural or man-made disasters, such as earthquakes and wars. (It must be stressed that we are speaking here of destruction in economic and not in physical terms.) Taken over a long period of time, the weight of this form of "consumption" is rather minimal. By far the most important case is the other one: the case in which consumption is a synonym for spending. If the field of observation—as taught in particular by the General Theory—is the national economy and not the individual person, then the major economic function of consumption is simply a *transfer of wealth*.[23]

Writing $S = Y - C$ and $S = I$, this economic function of consumption is, however, underplayed and perhaps even confused with the first. A superficial reading of the model would suggest this interpretation: the more spent on consumption, the less saved and the less available for investment. If this were the message of the General Theory it would have hardly elicited strong criticism from so many economists;[24] it would have hardly supported Keynes' hopes that he was writing a book which would "revolutionize" economic thinking.[25]

There also are in that model two implications of the concept of income defined as consumption plus investment which are worthy of note. With this definition Keynes fostered a trend to look forward which is not in full agreement with his belief that "...we have, as a rule, only the vaguest idea of any but the most direct consequences of our acts."[26] This consideration assumes a special significance if (a) this tendency to look forward is seen as giving great encouragement to economic planning,[27] and

---

[23] The precise definition of consumption in the *General Theory*, p. 62, is drawn in terms of sales. And a sale is only a transfer of wealth. (Also, income is in the same page precisely defined as total sales minus aggregate user costs of the entrepreneurs—with user cost including the concept of obsolescence, destruction, etc.; see pp. 23, 53-55, 58 and 66-73).

[24] *Cf.* Harris, Chapters III, IV and V, and esp. p. 29.

[25] *Cf.* Keynes' letter of January 1, 1935 to George Bernard Shaw quoted in Harrod, p. 462.

[26] Keynes, 1937a, p. 184.

[27] *Cf.* esp. Klein, Chapter VIII and p. 224.

(b) if economic planning is seen as a great departure from the classical tradition of primarily observing facts, events which have already happened and not venturing too far and too deep into the world of the future which—by definition—is unknown. The above has nothing to do with analysis and forecasting as agents which alter the future.

With income defined as consumption plus investment, the second implication is that there is a need to distinguish between consumption and investment. And yet, such a distinction must be arbitrary. As Keynes pointed out, "*Any* reasonable definition of the line between consumer-purchasers and investor-purchasers will serve us equally well, provided that it is consistently applied."[28]

Were Keynes' model (as well as the second generation of models which formally followed it) not used so much with the aim of arriving at predictions about the future but as a tool to understand the economic process—as Keynes undoubtedly intended it,—the arbitrary distinction between consumption and investment would not have direct practical consequences. This is not the case, however. Those models are used to make predictions about the future and influence economic policy, and that arbitrary distinction—coupled with the definitional problems of the concept of consumption—is bound to have an effect. The *autonomous* and *direct* impact which consumption has (or can have) on the economic process is bound to be discounted. The most famous historical case in point appears to have been the fate of the forecasts which were made toward the end of World War II. With the exception of W. S. Waytinsky, all other economists grossly misjudged the future.[29]

Finally, the concept of wealth in Keynes' model is largely left indeterminate.

In summary, all major definitions in Keynes' model seem to present some logical difficulties which can escape attention for a variety of reasons: (1) the concept of saving is made to perform a "passive" role; [30] (2) the flaws in the concept of investment are covered by its equivalence to the concept of saving; (3) the concepts of income and wealth are derivative concepts and therefore assume a secondary importance; (4) it is rare that consumption takes the major lead as the spur of the economic process.

---

[28] *General Theory*, p. 61. Italics added.
[29] Leijonhufvud, esp. p. 327 and Chapter III:2.
[30] Lekachman, p. 164.

Those flaws, however, are there and very few might deny that a model without those flows should be able to produce better results. We shall now attempt to reach new definitions of the same economic concepts and build a new model.

The starting point shall be the definition of income. Keynes, in fact, pointed out that this definition was one of the "three perplexities which most impeded (his) progress in writing" the *General Theory*.[31] This time we shall approach the task from the point of view of the consumer.

The first equation shall therefore be:
$$Y = C + S \tag{1}$$
where the symbols represent the same concepts as in Keynes' model, but their definitions and their relationships to each other are different.

The suggested equation of income is self-evident. It refers to the use to which income is put by the consumer.[32] And income must be either spent or saved. Only one objection can be raised against this equation. At first sight, it excludes investment from the field of observation. It shall be seen, however, that this objection is not valid in terms of the model we are trying to build. Investment shall be taken into account.

Before proceeding any further with the task of model building, let us pause to analyze the definition of a key concept included here, that of saving.

It seems that clarity of economic discourse would compel us to have a concept of saving which is independent of any other economic term. Such independent meaning, it is maintained here, can be reached only if saving is made to represent all wealth which can *neither be consumed nor can be confused with investment*. If this condition is accepted, then the concept of saving can be made to cover exclusively all forms of *unproductive wealth*—i.e., gold, unproductive land, jewels which are never worn, cash in a vault, etc. [To avoid confusion, the word "saving" was eventually substituted with the word "hoarding."]

These are all forms of wealth which can indeed be saved. *They do not lose any value over time.* On the contrary, since their carrying costs are either negligible or nil and

---

[31] Kaldor and Mirrlees, speaking of the characteristics of their model, stated, p. 166: "... like all 'Keynesian' economic models, it assumes that 'savings' are *passive*..." (Italics added).

[32] Johnson, p. 3; *General Theory*, p. 37.

since the history of the world is a history of inflation, with the exception of cash in a vault, these forms of wealth generally acquire value over time.

One of the chief benefits of writing $Y = C + S$ is the fostering of the immediate recognition that an increase in S improves one's balance sheet but it does not increase national wealth. An increase in savings ultimately does not even increase personal wealth; with saving defined as above and in the absence of inflation, saving can not even do that. In the final analysis, whatever gain is shown in the personal balance sheet at the end of the year has been acquired *at the expense of one's own* consumption and/or investment potential.

Another chief benefit of writing $Y = C + S$ might be the possibility of arriving at more precise forecasts of the future in periods which—like the current one (summer of 1974)—there seems to be a flight from productive investments and a strong tendency to "invest" in unproductive wealth as an edge against inflation.

Once the concept of saving is defined, investment becomes an equally very definite concept—i.e., all productive wealth, all wealth *which produces income, goods and services.*

Thus we have (almost) all the necessary elements to build the second equation in our model.

If the second equation of Keynes' model is maintained, one simply holds an empty and inoperative tautology. If one changes it to $I = Y - C$, one reaches the conclusion that $I = S$. This conclusion is untenable, not only because it reverses the problems mentioned in the previous section in relation to Keynes' model, but because—recalling the newly reached definition of saving—one would equate productive wealth to unproductive wealth. Neither can one conveniently introduce any other term—such as credit, for instance—to build the second equation.

Once the definition of saving is firmly established, preferably as suggested above, the second equation must inescapably be:
$$I = Y - S \tag{2}.$$
Combining (1) and (2), one reaches the conclusion that $I = C$. Before analyzing this new equivalence, let us focus our attention on the resulting definition of consumption.

Consumption, in accordance with the new model, is all wealth which is *used* either for the production of other goods or for direct enjoyment. The arbitrary distinction between investment and consumption mentioned above loses any practical or theoretical value. In the proposed model, $I \equiv C$.

$I \equiv C$ equivalence becomes intelligible as soon as one disaggregates C into consumption of consumer goods (let us say, C_c) and consumption of capital goods (C_k). The equivalence of I to C thus becomes: $I = C_c + C_k$.[33] (Or, more precisely, C $= C_c + C_k$ and $I = F_c + C_k$, where F_c stands for finished Consumer Products; and, since $F_c = C_c$, $I = C$.)

The equivalence of I to $C_c + C_k$ echoes the classical distinction between, respectively, "unproductive" and "productive" consumption. It immediately conveys the meaning attributed to consumption in the *General Theory*. It is "modern" in the sense that it gives to the *consumer* the role of prime mover in the economic system. (It is the consumer who decides to spend his income directly on consumer goods, or buys a plot of land, a house, a machine shop or even decides to hire a professional entrepreneur to look after his interests.)

This equivalence is also historically and logically correct. The first act of production—i.e., reaching for the apple (?) on the tree—must have been indistinguishable from an act of consumption. Today, in a money economy, this relationship should be even more evident: an act of production makes consumption possible; and consumption, in turn, creates anew the need for production. Indeed, in a money economy, with an act of consumption one does not only convey the message of a need for more production; one even *transfers* the financial resources which allow others to continue their productive activity and prosper.

Logically, there is no difference between an act of consumption and an act of investment. At least, entrepreneurs do not see any such difference. They look at other entrepreneurs as consumers—consumers just as the apple-eaters. They scan the market and produce, not in accordance with any such distinction, but in accordance with the availability of purchasing power which is ready to be spent, or, as Keynes would say, availability of "effective demand" in the market.[34] Certainly,

---

[33] In the 1937a article, Keynes wrote, p. 190: "... an increase in income will be divided in some proportion or another between spending and saving..." ($Y = C + S$).

[34] In the 1937a article, Keynes wrote, p. 190: "I say that effective demand is made up of two items—investment-expenditure ... and consumption-expenditure." ($I = C_c + C_k$).

neither duration of life nor ability to produce further wealth are inherent qualities of investment vs. consumption goods. Dried apples can outlast machines; one can make juice and tarts from apples.

The only difference between investment and consumption goods resides in their intended use: the former are used to produce further wealth (i.e., delayed and indirect consumption satisfaction); the latter are used to derive direct satisfaction and enjoyment. Yet, as far as use or "consumption" is concerned there is no difference here. Both types of goods are consumed.

Once the definitions of the three major concepts—i.e., consumption, investment, and saving—are accepted as valid, the definition of income as the sum of consumption and saving is also confirmed as valid. Indeed, using the disaggregate form of consumption, the definition of income becomes: $Y = C_c + C_k + S$. This definition, if seen as value of stocks and not as flow of funds, immediately yields a precise definition of wealth (W):

$$W = C_c + C_k + S.$$

This definition is in accordance with common wisdom which says: out of last year's income I consumed "x", invested "y", and saved "z".

It is believed that the proposed model does not only eliminate those flaws from Keynes' model which have been discussed above; it also makes the ideas expressed in the *General Theory* of more immediate apperception. The value of the proposed model, however, has not only an academic value; it does not only provide a new classification of economic terms and eventually make the exegesis of the General Theory relatively easier to expound. Rather, it is pleasant to believe, the value of this model resides in its application to economic theory and policy.

This model might give rise to a new Theory of Growth. Through the prism of the proposed model, it can immediately be seen that economic growth can occur not only through an exogenous influx of public investment—as in the end, due to the immediate circumstances, Keynes felt obliged to suggest. Economic growth can also occur through a reduction of private (as well as, indeed, public and corporate) savings [hoarding]. Thus, savings can be either invested or consumed: i.e., gold can be used for dentistry (?) and art, unused land for housing and recreation, etc. At the limit, with $S = 0$ the proposed model reads:

$$Y = C$$
$$I = Y$$
$$I = C.$$

Needless to say, increased investment—together with increased consumption—in "year" 1, is going to produce a bigger income in "year" 2. And, if the proportion of income spent on the two items (consumer goods and capital goods) is in relation to their respective production, there will not be any inflation.

Needless to say, implied here is not the economics of perfect calculations, ease, and abundance. There will always be errors in judgment. It will always take effort to produce wealth; and there will always be *temporary* limits to the economic process set not only by the availability of purchasing power and readiness to spend it, but also by the availability of human as well as natural/artificial resources.

The suggested adaptation of the proposed model to the Theory of Growth might also begin to give us a new understanding of the inflationary process. Here only the two crucial events in this process shall be outlined.

First, any purchase of unproductive wealth—even at the bottom of the recovery—is by definition inflationary. An amount of money is injected into the economy for which there is no correspondent increase of goods and services. The flow of the economic process is cut into two—with one half left frozen, or unproductive of further income and/or goods and services, and the second half fluctuating. This second half might be directed toward the purchase of more unproductive wealth. Then the negative effects of the action of the first marginal operator might become cumulative. Indeed, the entire process has to be seen over time as accompanying, or, perhaps better, itself constituting the business cycle. (At the bottom of the cycle, demand for unproductive wealth is almost zero; and the effective demand for productive wealth begins to grow. At the peak of the recovery, the composition of the aggregate demand function is reversed).

The second crucial event on which we shall lightly touch occurs toward the peak of the recovery, when the largest part of the flow of money still runs into productive wealth: investment outlets become scarcer, the marginal efficiency of capital decreases (or is believed to decrease), and "the" interest rate rises—not so much because the supply of money is somehow deficient as because its demand is abnormally high. This increased "liquidity preference," in turn, is due to a large number of factors some of which shall be listed below:

    a) the flow of money reverses its course (hence an increased demand for it) from investment goods back into comparatively scarce unproductive wealth; namely, savings or presumably *secure* wealth;

    b) the financial needs of the productive process must somehow be satisfied, and they will be satisfied through borrowing;

    c) financial fortunes are lost in the bear market;

    d) the price of unproductive wealth increases;

    e) the price of consumer goods also increases. With ongoing disinvestment and high interest rates, the productive process begins to provide less than the peak flow of such goods and services;

    f) the price of investment goods also increases, while their production decreases;

    g) less money income—both in the form of labor-income and of capital-income—is created and distributed;

    e) less revenue is received by the productive process because of a lower consumption rate.

These processes are, of course, largely circular in nature. They tend to reinforce each other. Certainly, not enough of the economic process has been observed here and not at sufficient depth to suggest any economic policy which might be followed in the presence of current events or at any other time. One general observation, however, might be warranted.

If the above propositions are deemed to possess any value, eventually they will unavoidably influence economic policy. There is certainly a great difference between a diagnosis—as Keynes' model suggests—that economic ills stem from a volatility of investment, and a diagnosis—as suggested by the proposed model—that economic ills stem from a cyclical desirability of unproductive wealth. The economic policy which flows (or should flow) from one diagnosis has to be different from the economic policy which flows (or should flow) from the other.

Concluding Comments

The issues dealt with here certainly deserve more attention than it was possible to give them. The main concern, however, was not the treatment of the many substantive issues as the desire to submit the proposed model to the evaluation of the academic community.

Obviously, a model is only a tool. By itself, it does not do any work. A better tool—as hopefully has been built here—only has the potential of assisting in doing better work. Ultimately, the value of the model must be judged in relation to the value of that amount of theoretical and empirical work which lies ahead.

In other words, what is requested of the academic community is to pass a partial and suspended judgment on the potential value of the proposed model.

References

A. H. Hansen, *Monetary Theory and Fiscal Policy*, New York 1949.

S. E. Harris, *The NewEconomics*, New York 1947.

R. F. Harrod, *The Life of John Maynard Keynes*, New York 1951.

F. A. Hayek, *The Road to Serfdom*, Chicago 1944.

H. G. Johnson, "The General Theory after Twenty-five Years," *Amer. Econ. Rev.* May 1961, Vol. LI, No. 2.

N. Kaldor and J. A. Mirrlees, "A New Model of Economic Growth," in F. H. Hahn, ed., *Readings in the Theory of Growth*, New York 1971.

J. M. Keynes, *A Treatise on Money*, 2 Vols., New York 1930.

______, *The General Theory of Employment, Interest, and Money*, New York 1936.

______, "The General Theory of Employment," *Quarterly Journal of Economics*, February 1937a, reprinted in S. E. Harris, ed., *op. cit.*

______, "Alternative Theories of the Rate of Interest," *The Economic Journal*, June 1937b.

L. R. Klein, *The Keynesian Revolution*, 2d ed., New York 1966.

A. Leijonhufvud, *On Keynesian Economics and the Economics of Keynes*, New York 1968.

R. Lekachman, *The Age of Keynes*, New York 1966.

A. P. Lerner, "Savings Equals Investment," reprinted in S. E. Harris, ed., *op. cit.*

P. Suppes, *Introduction to Logic*, Princeton 1957.

Chapter 3: Concordian economics: An Overall View

Einstein said,
"We cannot solve our problems with the same thinking we used when we created them."

Buckminster Fuller said,
"You never change things by fighting the existing reality. To change something, build a new model that makes the existing model obsolete."

At Proverbs 29:18 it is written:
"Where there is no vision, the people perish."

Introduction

Concordian economics is an integration of theory, policy, and practice. The theory integrates **Production** of real goods and services; **Consumption** or expenditure of financial assets to acquire real goods and services; and the **Distribution** of ownership rights over goods as well as money. The policy integrates the right to participate in the economic process (**participative justice**); (in order to obtain) the right to a fair share of what one produces (**distributive justice**); and the right to receive an equivalent value of what one gives (**commutative justice**). The practice integrates economic rights and responsibilities in relation to the four modern factors of production.

A Bit of History

Concordian economics was born in 1965, when, after a summer of intense intellectual struggle with the *General Theory*, the writer inserted Hoarding into Keynes' model of the economic system and found himself in a different cultural universe. The procedure is reproducible. We will all obtain the same result.

Once Upon a Time

Once upon a time economics was not a science; it was a practice. It was controlled by the principles of economic justice, principles that were enunciated by Aristotle and endorsed by Saint Thomas Aquinas. These principles remained undisputed for about two thousand years, basically until Adam Smith came along and gave us the "science" of economics. At the same time, from Moses, through Jesus of the Parable of the Talents, to the Doctors of the Church everyone knew about Hoarding.[1]

Today, without batting an eyelash, it is stated that "economics is what economists do." Trouble is economists do not seem able to agree what is that they do. A majority of them seem to be convinced that the science of economics is the study of the Market. Let us see.

The Behavior of the Market

Why do most mainstream economists believe, as Adam Smith did, that the Market is ruled by an *invisible hand* leading us gently to a condition of equilibrium and well-being?

The reason is that for most economists, as they openly admit, economics is a black box.

MANIPULATING the laws of demand (D) and supply (S), economists develop

theories of what should go in…   and observe what comes out:

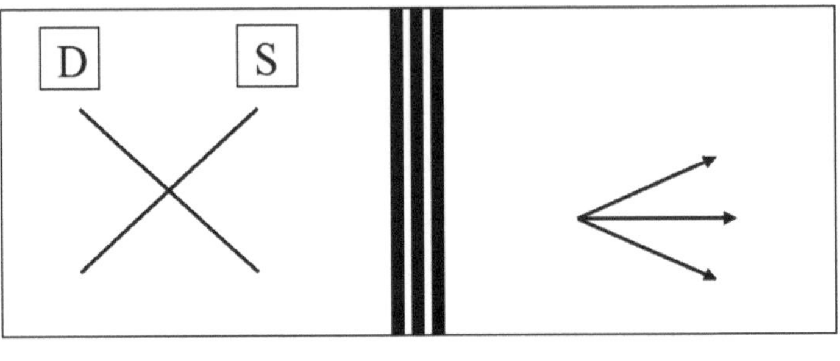

Fig. 1- INPUT   Fig. 2- OUTPUT

When analyzed in depth, the results of any theory, on the one hand, plausibly lead to growth; on the other, they lead to stability; and on the other they lead to decline.

Economists do not know what happens within the box.

Why?
The fundamental reason is that Saving was substituted for Hoarding by Adam Smith—and made "equal" to Investment. The proposition that Saving equals Investment is at the foundation of all modern economic theory.[2]

Trouble is Saving = Investment is a dogma. Neither Keynes nor any other economist has been able to explain why is Saving = Investment.[3]

And no one ever will because Saving in its incarnation as money deposited in a bank *is* Investment: It is the lowest form of investment.

We Need a New Paradigm

As a result of fifty years of in-depth analysis, which started with the (re)introduction of Hoarding in economic analysis, the writer has designed a set of tools that allow us to look inside the black box. Professor Franco Modigliani, a Nobel laureate in economics at MIT, and Professor M. L. Burstein, among many other experts in a variety of disciplines, have assisted this research, respectively for 27 and 23 years.

Inside the black box, one finds, not an economic theory but the operations of the Economic Process.

The Economic Process

As pointed out in a book,[4] which is now in its third edition, and in numerous papers published in peer-reviewed (albeit rather obscure) journals,[5] the central understanding of the Economic Process results from the integration of Production of real goods and services, the Distribution of ownership rights over real and monetary wealth, and Consumption or expenditure of monetary wealth to acquire real wealth. Even in the sale of a car, we have these three items: car, money, and deed of ownership. This is true theory: It is an accurate description of facts.

Logically, these elements are tied together in a relation of equivalence:

$$\text{Production} \leftrightarrow \text{Distribution} \leftrightarrow \text{Consumption.}$$

Production, Distribution, and Consumption are not single words. They are concepts. They form processes of their own. Their integration can be seen at a glance in the following figure—and its mirror image that represents economic policy:

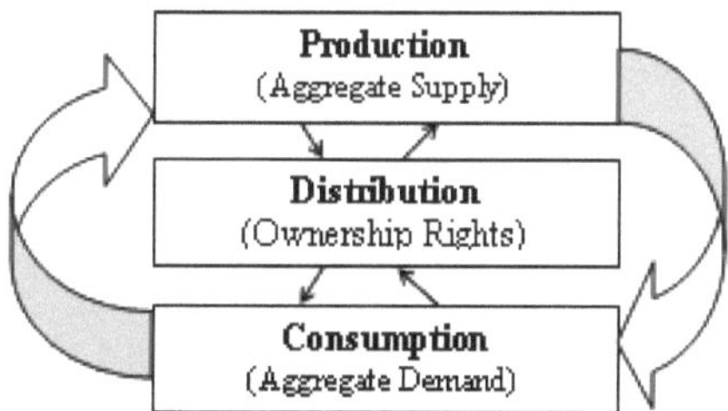

Fig, 3- Economic Theory – The Economic Process

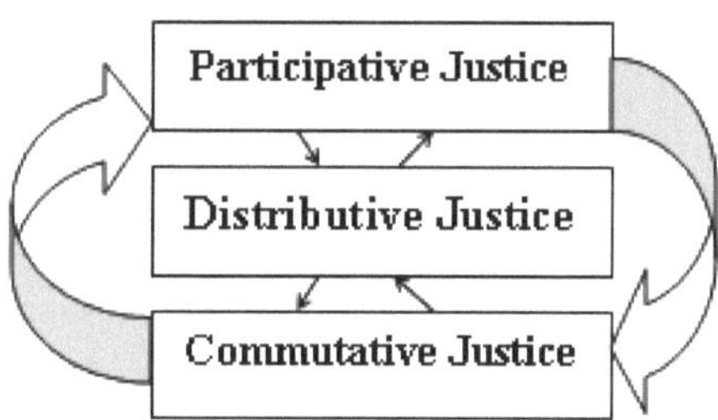

Fig, 4- Economic Policy – Economic Justice

Figure 3 catches the economic process at the moment of the exchange. It indicates that a cycle of the economic process is completed when the entire production of the period is sold. Then an exchange has occurred between money and goods. For the exchange to take place, both the producer and the buyer, in an ordered society, must be legal owners of the wealth they exchange.

Placing Figure 4 next to Figure 3, we realize that this construction of the economic process is nothing new! It is simply a **return** to the millenarian concern with economic justice, which from Aristotle to the present has been understood as composed of "distributive" justice and "commutative" justice. Concordian economics allows us to put the capstone on this construction: "Participative" justice. The economic process is nothing but the mirror image of the complete description of three essential principles of economic justice.

Participative Justice offers a one-to-one correspondence with the production process; Distributive Justice a one-to-one correspondence with the process of distribution of ownership rights over real and monetary wealth; Commutative Justice gives us a one-to-one correspondence with the consumption process or the process of expenditure of monetary wealth to acquire real wealth.

Economic justice keeps the economic process in equilibrium to the benefit of all. Economic injustice keeps the market in disequilibrium to the detriment of all. Short term benefits to the few from injustice are ephemeral. An overview of long term trends makes these relationships quite clear.

A Geometric Representation of Economic Dynamics

Starting from an equilibrium condition at time 0, the geometric representation of economic dynamics of Production, Distribution, and Consumption—here represented respectively as values of real wealth (RW), values of distribution of ownership (DO) rights, and values of monetary wealth (MW)—is as follows:

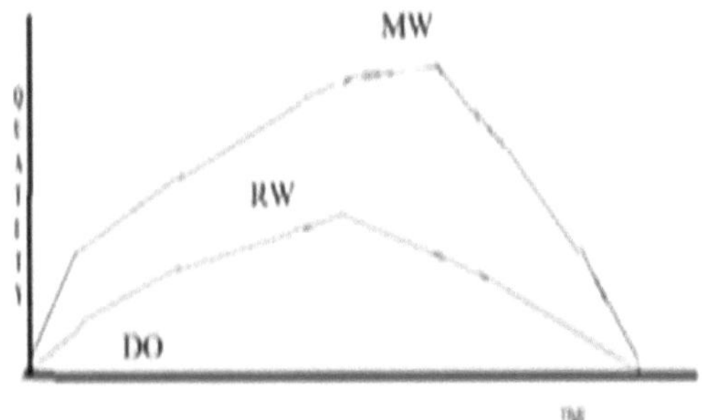

Fig. 5- The economic process over time

This figure suggests that, since they are relatively easier to create, the rate of growth of assets composing monetary wealth (MW) is faster than the rate of growth of assets composing the category of real wealth (RW). And then there is the problem of the accelerating pace of concentration of the distribution of ownership (DO) rights into a few hands—a phenomenon which at first cut is here assumed to be constant. Clearly, when monetary wealth is concentrated into a few hands, not enough money will be available to the majority of the population. The necessary equilibrium conditions implied in the P $\leftrightarrow$ D $\leftrightarrow$ C equivalence for the economic process as a whole, as represented in Figure 3, is broken and the process will not proceed organically forward.

Indeed, a bubble is created. The economic bubble is clearly visible from Figure 5: A bubble is a separation of monetary wealth from real wealth and is measured by the area between MW and RW. As pointed out elsewhere, in Concordian economics these values are kept separate and distinct from each other by defining them respectively as p-values (for values of the real economy), c-values (for values of the monetary economy), and d-values (for values of the legal economy or values of ownership rights).

How can equilibrium be restored?

Let us Look at Market Governance—Again

Following the dynamics implicit in Figure 5, it is possible to see how the Market might not always be ruled by a benign invisible hand. On occasion, the Market, left to the natural inclinations of ordinary human beings, is governed by another dictum by Adam Smith that is also in the *Wealth of Nations*. This is a less famous observation, but more pertinent to our situation today: "All for ourselves and nothing for other people, seems, in every age of the world, to have been the vile maxim of the masters of mankind."

If we are not misled by reductionist thinking of minds accustomed to analyzing linear trends only, we discover not one but **four** horses of inequality wandering all over the lot and leaving behind, instead of simple geometric patterns, a filigree of incredibly subtle interrelationships.

Four Horses of Inequality

Four horses of inequality raise their demanding heads as soon as one looks into the component elements of the Production Process. To produce anything, in a modern economy, one needs **control** over (1) Land and natural resources; (2) Tools in the form of physical capital as in plants and equipment; (3) Money in the form of financial capital; and, (4) Labor in its variegated manifestations of manual labor, intellectual labor, and (spiritual?) labor as in entrepreneurial leadership. These are the modern **factors** of production. It is only natural that human beings should attempt to get as much control as they can over each one of these factors. Inequality ensues.

Control over the factors of production has never been and never will be distributed equally among all human beings. That is a false, misleading, and dangerous ideal. Within limits, inequality is natural. No two snow flakes are alike. Human beings, as well as specific plots of land, are endowed by our Creator with different measures of qualities and quantities. It is natural that we are going to get unequal results.

What we need, and what the world stands for, is equality of opportunity.

Rights vs. Privileges

Access to the factors of production today is acquired as a privilege and naturally leads to unbridled inequality. The four horses of inequality are these four unbridled privileges:

- ✓ Privileged access to land and natural resources;
- ✓ Privileged access to money;
- ✓ Privileged access to the labor of others;
- ✓ Privileged access to the wealth of others.

Each one of these privileges—historically rooted mostly in plunder and conquest— has to be turned into a universal right **for everyone**, if we want to build a just and ordered society. We can then forget the past, and concentrate on the present and the future.

The opportunity is ours. We only need to realize that, while privileges divide, rights unite. Rights unite because they are born out of the exercise of corresponding responsibilities.

Four Economic Rights and Responsibilities

1. The right of access to land and natural resources	*1. Pay taxes on land and natural resources that are under our control*
2. The right of access to financial resources imbued in national credit	*2. Repay loans obtained through access to national credit*
3. The right of access to the fruits of one's labor	*3. Perform tasks required in the process of wealth creation*
4. The right of access to the fruits of one's property	*4. Respect the property of others.*

No other economic rights or responsibilities seem to be essential. The consistent assumption of these four responsibilities is all that can and ought to be ingrained into government policies—at various levels. These four policies, *gradually* pursued, will yield all the certainty and economic security that we need, because they foster structural changes that create conditions of economic freedom and justice for all. As an unearned consequence, the need for Hoarding will almost be rooted out of existence. A fringe of misers will always be with us. But when the majority of the population does not copy the miser, the damage will be minuscule.

Who Are the Opponents?

Who are the powerful people who would object to this program of action? Four presumed antagonists are supposed to be (1) landowners who do not want to pay their fair share of taxes on the value of their land; (2) central bankers who do not want to serve the public interest; (3) entrepreneurs who do not want to offer full compensation for services received; and (4) business people who want to gobble up the fruit of other people's effort.

Where are they? Apart from their miniscule apparitions, when measured against the billions of entrepreneurs who behave morally, they are **four phantoms**—but more dangerous for being ingrained in the imagination of people who, blinded by their institutional power, see neither economics nor morality clearly. READ: tax assessors, politicians, and academicians who, unable to speak truth to power, make themselves powerless and paralyze entire nations.

Serving Four Masters

You might think that this writer is a lone ranger roaming these vast expanses of economic territory—all alone. Nothing could be farther from the truth. He has consistently been serving four Masters of Economics. Four great American Masters of Economics. Forget Keynes… Forget Hayek.

For the control of land and natural resources, we all ought to be devoted servants of Henry George. By the way, mirabile dictu, do you know that not one but 8 Nobel laureates in economics endorsed Henry George's prescription to tax the value of the land…….while **reducing** taxes on buildings and, eventually, income?

For the control of money, with its relevant inscription into Article 1, Section 8 of the US Constitution, we all ought to be devoted servants of Benjamin Franklin.
For the control over the fruits of one's labor, we all ought to be devoted servants of Louis O. Kelso.

For the control over such basic industrial tools as the corporations (physical capital), we all ought to be devoted servants of Louis. D. Brandeis. The writer actually did his dissertation at the University of Naples on the political thought of Louis D. Brandeis; his work was awarded a Council of Europe Scholarship; and he entered the academic awards wind tunnel, in which he even caught a Fulbright Scholarship.

Conclusion

This is not "my" vision, says the writer. He does not claim originality. This is the vision that unfolds mathematically by inserting Hoarding, the core of the Parable of the Talents, into the structure of economic theory.

Once the root source of Concordian economics became clear to this writer in 2006 (!), to analyze what else did Jesus, Moses, and St. Thomas Aquinas thought about economics became an intellectual necessity.[6] That is a train of thought, explored mainly on the pages of Mother Pelican, that has led to the conclusion that there is no such thing as religion without economics and ultimately to a book titled The Centrality of the Resurrection. Thus Concordian economics is on At the cusp of some serious cultural developments.

Orwell might say that perhaps the most important long-term contribution of Concordian economics is to bring the language of economics in line with the language of common mortals. Stated more directly, Concordian economics adds clarity and reduces possibilities of corruption in the daily interface between economics, politics, and culture.

True, the econometrics of Concordian economics are still missing. They will come as soon as official data are collected in accordance with the specific categories of thought of the new paradigm. For the time being, this lacuna is not too worrisome. Apart from overwhelming factual evidence about the dangerousness of decisions taken on the basis of econometric models, thanks to Philip Pilkington, the readers of *Econintersect* have been recently reminded that neither Keynes nor Hicks placed much trust in current mainstream econometrics.[7]

Perhaps, this is a worthwhile New Year resolution to make. Let us abandon the dangerous misconceptions of mainstream economics. Let us wholeheartedly plunge into the new/old world of Concordian economics.

Notes

1.   Carmine Gorga, 2014. "Economics of Morality" at www.researchgate.net/publication/267569298_Economics_of_Morality.

2.   John Maynard Keynes, 1936. *The General Theory of Employment, Interest, and Money*. NY: Harcourt, p. 36.

3.   At p. 328, this is what Keynes (*op. cit*) said: A "view" which considers that saving is *not* equal to investment is "more usually supported by arguments which have no foundation at all apart from confusion of mind." This I took to be not a scientific explanation, but a dogma.

4.   Carmine Gorga, 2002. *The economic process: An instantaneous non-Newtonian Picture*. Lanham, Md. and Oxford: University Press of America. Third expanded paperback edition 2016. For reviews, see http://www.carmine-gorga.us/id18.htm.

5.   See, esp. Carmine Gorga, 2009. "Concordian Economics: Tools to Return Relevance to Economics." *Forum for Social Economics*, vol. 38, issue 1, pages 53-69.

6.   The economic profession is waking up to the need to analyze many aspects of the relationship between economics and religion. See, Shiya Iyer, "The New Economics of Religion." *Journal of Economic Literature* 2016, 54(2), 395-441. Yet, because of ideology and political correctness perhaps, the analysis of the economic content of religions is still missing from academic investigations.

7.   See, e.g., Daniel W. Drezner, "The state of macroeconomics is not good." *Washington Post*, September 15, 2016.

Chapter 4: Concordian Economics on the transformation of the "dismal science" of economics into The Economics of JUBILATION

Abstract

This paper offers the bare bones of the logic, non-linear mathematics, and fractal geometry used in the transformation of the "dismal science" of economics into The Economics of Jubilation.

Acknowledgments

The framework of analysis on which this paper draws is uniquely due to 27 years of exhaustive probing by Franco Modigliani and 23 years of assistance from Meyer L. Burstein. Mitchell S. Lurio and Norman G. Kurland have been great teachers of economic policy. This paper is especially due to editing assistance form Ralph Cole Waddey and reassuring guidance by Dr. Damon Cummings, Dr. Michael E. Brady, and Dr. Veljko Milutinovic.

1. INTRODUCTION

If Keynes (1936, pp. vi-vii) was right in stating that the key problem with the economic theory of his day was the neglect of money in its analysis, we can reasonably rest assured we are right in assuming that the key problem with the economic theory of our days is its neglect of real wealth. This oscillation between extremes is one of the reasons why economic theory remains a "dismal science"; there are many others; and they compel us to abandon the mainstream framework of analysis (cf. Gorga, 2010a). The best solution to this state of affairs is offered by the transformation of mainstream economics into The Economics of Jubilation.

The Economics of Jubilation is a new framework of analysis in which not only money and real wealth but also the ownership of wealth are recognized as essential elements of the economic system (Gorga, 2002, 2006 [2009], 2008a, and 2010b).

With the assistance of basic tools of logic, mathematics, and geometry in this paper we shall see how mainstream economics is transformed into the Economics of Jubilation.

2. FINDINGS

Keynes' model of the economic system (Keynes, 1936, p. 63) reads as follows:

$$\text{Income} = \text{Consumption} + \text{Investment}$$
$$\text{Saving} = \text{Income} - \text{Consumption}$$
$$\text{Saving} = \text{Investment.}$$

A detailed analysis (see, Gorga, 2002, pp. 41-57, 79-82, 93-103, 139-153) reveals that this model, the model on which mainstream economics is built, does not respect any of the fundamental principles of logic such as the principle of identity, the principle of non-contradiction, or the principle of equivalence. Here suffice it to report that in the calculation of R. W. Goldsmith (1955-1956, Vol. II, p. 69n) the definition of saving can assume 100,000 possible meanings. And the geometry of mainstream economics is widely acknowledged to be a "black box" (see, e.g., Petrongolo and Pissarides, 2001).

3. SOLUTIONS

The simplest method to transform Keynes' model into a system of thought that respects basic principles of logic is to rotate the model 360^0 around investment (Gorga, 2002, pp. 129-130). In this fashion:

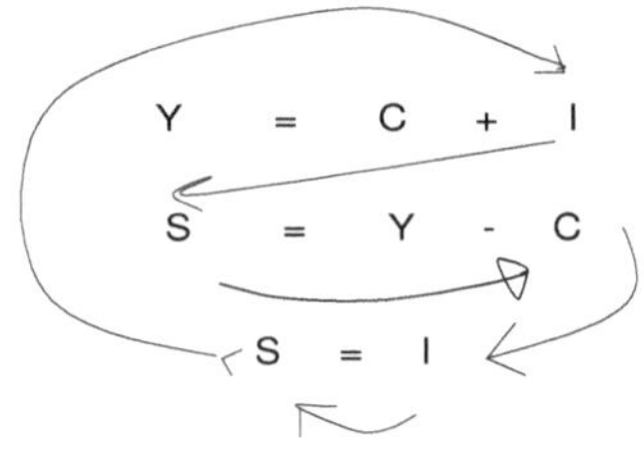

Figure 1. Pivoting Keynes' Model.

One then obtains the following Flows Model, the foundational model of Concordian economics (Gorga, 2002, 2008a, and 2010b):

$$\text{Income} = \text{Consumption} + \text{Saving (or Hoarding)}$$
$$\text{Investment} = \text{Income} - \text{Saving (or Hoarding)}$$
$$\text{Investment} = \text{Consumption}.$$

A brief account of this transformation is as follows. Since in mainstream economics saving equals investment, the first equation of the Flows Model is the same as the first equation of Keynes' model; but the meaning of terms is completely different. Consumption in Concordian economics means, not expenditure on consumer goods as in mainstream economics, but expenditure *tout court* and thus covers all types of expenditure. And saving means hoarding—wealth, whether real or monetary, that, in M. L. Burstein precise phrase, has zero use rate. It is the second equation of the new model that appears to be entirely new. Upon analysis, however, it turns out to be perhaps the first equation ever written in economics. It is nothing but the mathematical formulation of the Parable of the Talents, a parable that expresses the very core of the economics of Jesus—a system of economic thought that is a reformulation and a continuation of the economics of Moses (see, Gorga, 2006 [2009]).

Transferring the Parable of the Talents into a Lorenz diagram, one obtains:

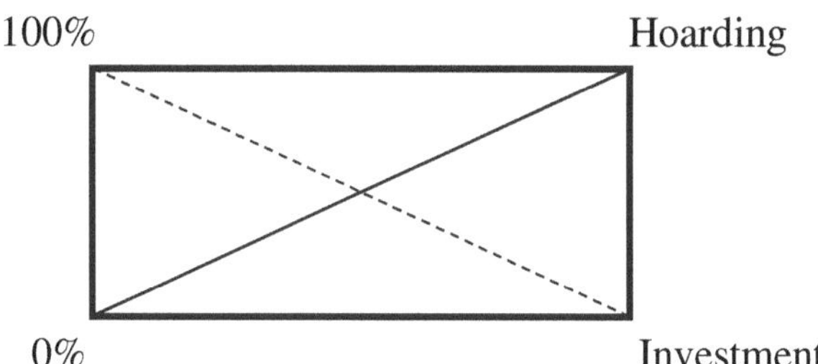

Figure 2. The Parable of the Talents.

This presentation of the Parable of the Talents helps us state in no uncertain terms that (1) more hoarding, less investment, hence less economic growth; (2) more hoarding of real wealth, more money in circulation that does not correspond to wealth, hence more inflation; (3) more wealth hoarded by the few, more poverty for the many. For details, see Gorga (2002, pp. 235-302, 329-353).

The third equation of the Flows Model, Investment = Consumption, allows us to define **Investment** unequivocally as production of real wealth and **Consumption** as expenditure of money. From which it follows that Investment is only and always investment, hence it respects the dictates of principle of identity and the principle of non-contradiction; ditto for Consumption, which is only and always consumption. Is Investment *equivalent* to Consumption?

Linking the two components of this equation to each other through the Distribution of ownership rights over real and monetary wealth, one transforms the third equation of Concordian economics into the following equivalence:

$$\text{Production} \leftrightarrow \text{Distribution} \leftrightarrow \text{Consumption.}$$

Thus Concordian economics does not only respect fundamental principles of logic, it also automatically separates real wealth form monetary wealth; and, as distinguished from classical economics and Keynesian economics, it includes them both in its analysis. In addition, it places the Distribution of ownership rights over real and monetary wealth at the very core of its analysis.

The equivalence of production to distribution to consumption can be better appreciated placing it into a geometric format. Thus:

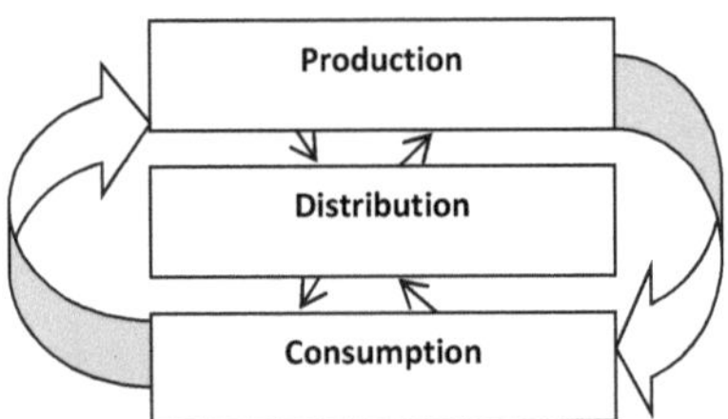

Figure 3. The Economic Process.

As distinguished from the "black box" of mainstream economics, the geometry of Concordian economics allows us to observe the inner mechanisms of the economic process as a whole. Figure 3 reads as follows. When goods and services pass from the producer to the consumer, money passes form the consumer to the producer. Both money and real wealth change hands in an exchange; and for this to occur, they must be both rightfully owned by the transactors. Hence, the observation of the economic consequences of the phenomenon of distribution of ownership rights that occur at the very core of economic analysis is not only a legal but an economic necessity.

Needless to say, Production, or Aggregate Supply, is a complex process in itself that is better analyzed in a disaggregated form. Ditto for Distribution and Consumption. Using Poincaré sections of Figure 3, we construct the following models:

Model of Production (P)

$$P = CG + KG + GH$$
$$KG = P - (GH + CG)$$
$$KG = OKG$$

where
CG stands for Consumer Goods
KG for Capital Goods
GH for Goods Hoarded
OKG for value of Ownership of Capital Goods

Model of Distribution (D)

$$D = OCG + OKG + OGH$$
$$OKG = D - (OGH + OCG)$$
$$OKG = I$$

where
D stands for Distribution or Real Income observed from the point of view of distribution of ownership rights
OCG for value of Ownership of Consumer Goods
OKG for value of Ownership of Capital Goods
OGH for value of Ownership of Goods Hoarded

Model of Consumption (C)

$$C = E_h + E$$
$$I = C - E_h$$
$$I = E$$

where

C stands for Consumption or Money Income observed
from the point of view of consumption
E_h for money reserved for Hoarding-Expenditure
E for money reserved for Expenditure (on consumer goods and capital goods)
I for Investment

Synthetic Model of the Economic System as a Whole
(see, e.g., Thompson, 1986, p. 36)

$$p^{\cdot} = fp(p,d,c)$$
$$d^{\cdot} = fd(p,d,c)$$
$$c^{\cdot} = fc(p,d,c)$$

where

$p^{\cdot}$ stands for rate of change in total production
$d^{\cdot}$ for rate of change in the values of distribution of ownership rights
$c^{\cdot}$ for rate of change in total expenditure.

Again, geometry can be of tremendous assistance to see the complexity of the economic system as a whole. Combining the result of Poincaré sections of each of the three component elements of Figure 3, we obtain:

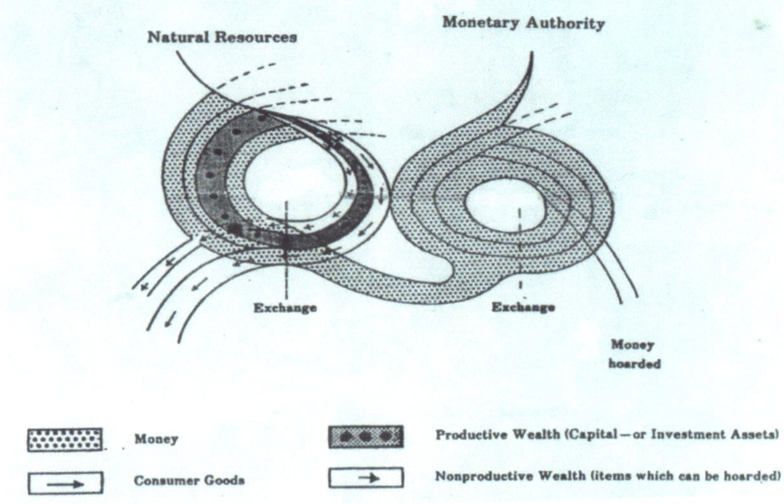

Figure 4. Flows of Values.

Physicists and mathematicians are accustomed to seeing this figure as a "strange attractor" (see, e.g., Mandelbrot, 1983, esp. pp. 193-99). This writer looks forward to the day in which data will either confirm or deny the validity of the assumption that the economic system behaves like any other biological and physical system as observed through the lenses of chaos theory.

Then, assisted by the following longitudinal analysis of Figure 3, as it can be seen from the following figure (see, Gorga, 2008b) it might even be possible to define and measure the "bubble" as the degree of separation of the trend line of Monetary Wealth (MW) from the trend line of Real Wealth (RW):

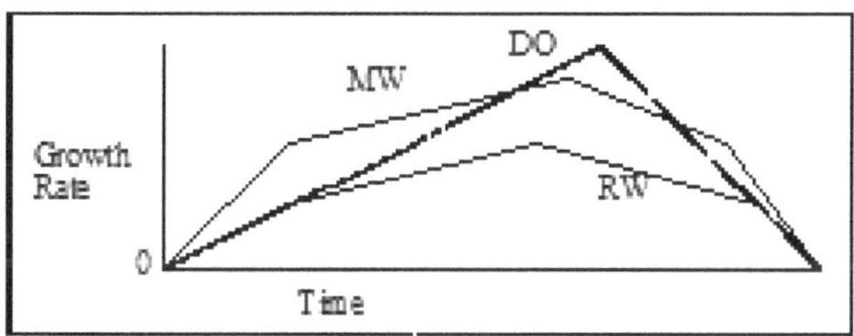

Figure 5. Trajectories of the System as a Whole.

Clearly, to reduce effects of the bubble on the shortest possible timetable and bring the trend line of real wealth in full alignment with the trend line of monetary wealth is a question of control—a question of creating a just and sustainable economy.

For this purpose, recourse to the ancients is again invaluable. In this search, one meets the economic discourse that was carried out from Moses and Aristotle to the Doctors of the Church on the wave of the doctrine of economic justice, which was composed of distributive justice and commutative justice. One simply needs to add to it the plank of participative justice and transform it into the theory of economic justice (see Gorga, 1999). Thus:

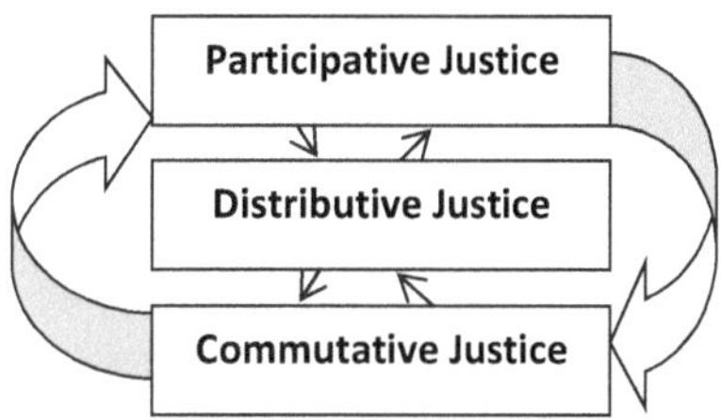

Figure 6. Economic Justice

As it can be seen, Figure 6 is the shadow of Figure 3. Observed side to side, these two figures make it clear that one can just as soon separate the economic process from the theory and practice of economic justice as one can separate a person from her shadow.

The question then becomes how can we introduce the wisdom of the ages into the complexity of the modern world? Detailed analysis indicates that the following four economic rights and responsibilities will go a long way toward reaching this goal (see, e.g., Gorga 2008a):

1. We all have the right of access to natural resources—and the responsibility to pay taxes for the exclusive use of those resources;

2. We all have the right of access to national credit—and the responsibility to repay loans obtained on the basis of national credit;

3. We all have the right to the fruits of our labor—and the responsibility to offer services equal to the value of our compensation;

4. We all have the right to protect our wealth—and the responsibility to respect the wealth of others.

4. CONCLUSION

The transformation of mainstream economics into the Economics of Jubilation allows us to integrate all key elements of the economic process and eventually will allow us to get a better control of economic events.

References

Goldsmith, Raymond W. 1955-1956. *A Study of Saving in the United States,* 3 vols.; Princeton, NJ: Princeton University Press.

Gorga, Carmine. 1999. "Toward the Definition of Economic Rights," *J. Markets and Morality,* 2:1, pp. 88-101.*

______ . 2002. *The Economic Process: An Instantaneous Non-Newtonian Picture.* Lanham, MD and Oxford: University Press of America.

______ . 2006 [2009]. "The Economics of Jubilation - Blinking Adam's Fallacy Away". Available at SSRN: http://ssrn.com/abstract=1489570.

______ . 2008a. "Concordian Economics: Tools to Return Relevance to Economics", *Forum for Social Economics,* www.springerlink.com, May.*

______ . 2008b. "Economics for Physicists and Ecologists," *Transactions on Advanced Research* January, Vol. 4 (1) 6-9.
http://internetjournals.net/journals/tar/IPSI%20TAR%20Jan%202008.pdf

______. 2010a (forthcoming). "From the Dismal Science to the Economics of Jubilation." *In* Frank Columbus, ed., *Economic Theory.* Hauppauge, NY: Nova Science Publishers.

______. 2010b (fortcoming). *The Economic Process: An Instantaneous Non-Newtonian Picture.* Lanham, MD and Oxford: University Press of America. A paperback expanded edition.

Keynes, J. Maynard. 1936. *The General Theory of Employment, Interest, and Money.* NY: Harcourt.

Mandelbrot, Benoit, B. 1983. *The Fractal Geometry of Nature.* New York: Freeman.
Petrongolo, Barbara and Pissarides, Christopher A. 2001. "Looking into the Black Box: A Survey of the Matching Function," *Journal of Economic Literature,* Vol. XXXIX, p. 424.

Thompson, J. M. T. (1986). *Nonlinear Dynamics and Chaos, Geometric Methods for Engineers and Scientists*. New York: Wiley.

* These essays are reprinted in Gorga, Carmine. 2009. *To My Polis, With Love: May Gloucester Show the World the Ways of Frugality*. Gloucester, MA: The Somist Institute.

Chapter 5: THE ECONOMICS OF JUBILATION
Blinking Adam's Fallacy Away

Abstract

A system of thought allowed for the free market price of land to cyclically go down to zero. This is the economics of Moses. The economics of Jesus is a restatement of the economics of Moses. The first was applied during Biblical times and the latter, united with Aristotle's thought and transformed by the Doctors of the Church into the doctrine of economic justice, was applied over vast territories up until the late Renaissance. With the assistance of Concordian economics, the mathematization of the Parable of the Talents leads to an opportunity to adapt those two ancient economic perspectives to the complexity of the modern world. In so doing one blinks Adam's Fallacy and the subsequent mainstream economics away.

Acknowledgments

The framework of analysis on which this paper draws is uniquely due to 27 years of exhaustive probing by Franco Modigliani and 21 years of assistance from Meyer L. Burstein. Mitchell S. Lurio and Norman G. Kurland have been great teachers of economic policy. Technical assistance was offered by Charles F. Schibener, III. Much encouragement was continuously provided by Alan Reynolds, Raymond G. Torto, and John K. Skank. Otto Eckstein, Frank L. Cooper, Steve H. Hanke, and Harry G. Johnson were the first economists to confirm that the revised Keynes' model was consistent. I also would like to acknowledge a clarification brought to this paper by Godfrey Dunkley. Helpful comments, suggestions, and recommendations on earlier drafts of this paper were tendered by a number of referees as well as by William J. Baumol, Michele Boldrin, Jeroen C.J.M. van den Bergh, Kevin P. Gallagher, William J. Toth, William R. Collier, Jr., Michael Emmett Brady, and Myron S. Geller. Selective portions of this analysis have also been endorsed by John K. Galbraith, Mark Perlman, Francesco Forte, Augusto Graziani, Alberto Tarchiani, Aldo Garosci, Giorgio Spini, Gerald Alonzo Smith, Charles T. Wood, Norman A. Bailey, Buckminster Fuller, Rosanna Marini, Gordon Richards, Rudy Oswald, Steve Kurtz, Ernest Kahn, Louis J. Ronsivalli, Howard Zinn, Robert F. Drinan, Thomas J. Marti, Cassian J. Yuhaus, James E. Hug, Richard John Neuhaus, John J. Neuhauser, Irving Kristol, Michael J. Naughton, and John C. Rao among others. Thanks for editorial assistance go to Jonathan F. Gorga and David S. Wise.

Analysis reveals the existence of a body of doctrines that can be properly classified as the economics of Moses and the economics of Jesus: a delicate balance of economic rights and economic responsibilities. Astounding as this proposition sounds at first hearing, these perspectives shed a unique light on about three thousand years of economic literature and practice. To appreciate the inner coherence of this body of doctrines, it is necessary to treat them separately. Part I of this paper attempts to reconstruct the economics of Moses; Part II the economics of Jesus. Part III presents conditions through which these doctrines can be interjected into the complexities of the modern world.

The economics of Moses is contained in two fundamental doctrines: *Observe Jubilee* (including Sabbath and Sabbatical year) and *Do Not Steal*. The first is enunciated in Ex 20:8-11; 34:21; Lev 23:3; 25:2-16, 23-28; Num 33:53-54; 34; and Deut 5:12-15; 15:1; the second in Ex 20:15 and Deut 5:19. We shall see that these two doctrines embrace the whole of economics.

The economics of Jesus is a restatement of the economics of Moses and is contained in three fundamental doctrines. Two complementary doctrines are derived from the Parable of the Talents in Mt 25:14-30: The first doctrine states, *Invest Your Talents*; the second states, *Do Not Hoard*. The third is enunciated in Mt 22:21: *Give to Caesar What Is Caesar's*. We shall see that these three doctrines contain the whole of economics.

Both sets of doctrines contain the whole world of economics, because—rather than starting from the economics of the household, as the Greeks did—they both address the whole of the economic process, which, as established by Classical economists, contains, not the market exchange of two commodities, but the study of the production, distribution, and consumption of wealth of an entire nation or the world as a whole. Of course, both Moses and Jesus explain theory and policy in accordance with the exigencies of the historic moment of their time. Hence, what changes is not the substance of the discourse but the response to immediate needs and the literary expression. As we shall see, the content of the doctrine of the Jubilee is the same as the content of the doctrine of Not Hoarding; and the content of the doctrine of Not Stealing is the same as the content of the doctrine of Giving to Caesar what is

Caesar's. In Moses the injunction to invest is implicit; in Jesus this injunction is explicit.

The reason for the last difference becomes clear when it is placed in the context of modern economic theory. From Adam Smith (if not from Locke or even the late scholastics) onward, it has become axiomatic that freedom is a condition of economic growth. Give people economic freedom, and moral, normal people will invest their talents in the most productive way that is open to them. The operation of the butcher and the baker, the creation of a symphony, just as the creation of a useful gadget or a financial derivative, are included in the use to which God-given freedom (see esp. Gen 3:22; Ex 8:1-32; and Gal 5:13) can be put in our world. From which one must deduce, and history confirms, that by the time of Jesus people had lost most of their natural economic freedom. Hence Jesus had to make explicit the need to invest one's talents.

Naturally, both Moses and Jesus are deeply concerned with the condition of the poor, the marginalized, those who—for any reason—are excluded from the blessings and burdens of participating in the economic process. We shall see that giving to the poor is an implicit aspect of the Jubilee and an explicit aspect of the doctrine of not hoarding. Yet, giving to the poor is not an economic doctrine; it is a moral injunction. Transfers of wealth from the rich to the poor, just as transfers from the poor to the rich, do not form an economic doctrine. They are moral—or immoral— practices: They are moral, if voluntary; they are immoral, if involuntary and forced. Unrecorded, there is much voluntary giving from poor to poor and from the poor to the rich, which the rich are always willing to accept. Such is the way among human beings.

Part I — The Economics of Moses

The two economic doctrines of Moses are: *Observe Jubilee*; *Do Not Steal*.

1. Observe Jubilee

What is the doctrine of the Jubilee? There are many facets to this doctrine which lie outside the scope of this paper (cf. Harris 1996; Trocmé 1973). Our focus is on its economic content. This is an economic doctrine and practice of subtle complexity. There are three aspects to it: one concerns land; the other concerns money; the third concerns products-things-time.

Jubilee Concerning Land

Economists might want to study the medium term injunction of the Jubilee, liberally extended to cover the Sabbatical and everyday practices. This is the injunction to leave the land fallow every seven years—to let it organically rest so that it will recover its powers naturally, rather than force feeding it with chemicals. (Because of the savings involved in any reduction of chemicals and smaller external costs of clearing the effects of chemicals from the waters downstream and eventually the water table, economists may wish to give this practice more than a fleeting glance. The appetite for the economics of pesticides might be wetted by the knowledge that pesticides—while harming human health and the ozone layer—are used, not to enhance the productivity of the land, as to eliminate blemishes from the produce appearance.) Here we are concerned with the long term economic—and, necessarily, legal and moral—aspects of the Jubilee in relation to the land. By the end of the 49th year, the doctrine calls for the return of the land to the original possessor. Hence, on the 50th year—the Jubilee year—the slate is clean. Just as with the U.S. Homestead Act of 1862 or in the Amish community and Bali today, the original possessor acquires land at no cost (Num 33:53-54; 34), a gift from inheritance. The responsibility is to till the land. The purely economic aspects of the Jubilee are revealed by the practice of purchase and sale of land during the forty-nine years preceding the Jubilee; by the existence of price; and by the existence of market. These three aspects are coordinated to such an extent that, with passage of time, the price of the land—astonishingly—goes progressively *down* to zero the closer one gets to the year of the Jubilee (see Lev 25:13-16; 27:16-24). These three aspects bear deep examination. And they can be better understood by indirection. Purchase and sale of land could have been prohibited; and there would have been no market, and thus no price. The price mechanism of the Jubilee calls for close attention. Since the price of land decreases with the passage of time, the arrangement reveals that there was the observation of an inner coordination of events in the application of the Jubilee: first, everyone obeyed the mechanism; since there is no evidence of compulsion, everyone obeyed it voluntarily; and since the price of the land decreased over time, it was clearly responding to a framework of economic analysis. What was this framework? The process of price determination becomes reproducible and decipherable as one looks at the economic, the legal, and the moral context into which the purchase and sale of land was taking place.

The Economic Context. To see the various relationships involved in the institution of the Jubilee, it is useful to build the following analytic framework:

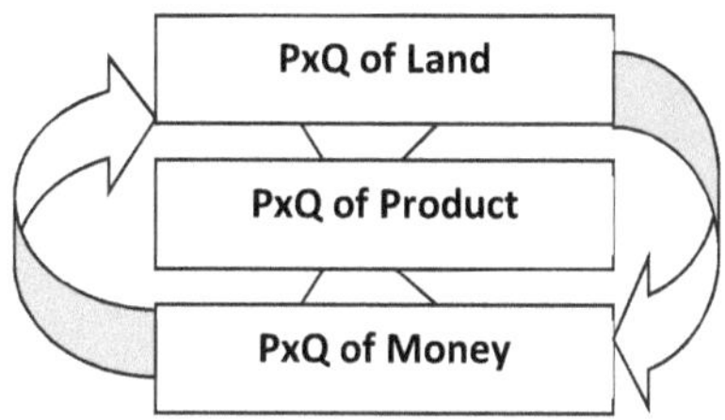

*Figure*1. A Framework of Economic Analysis

The process of price determination for the land established an equivalence (see e.g., Allen 1970, p. 748)— in conditions of equilibrium, a *constant* one to one relation— among three elements: price times quantity of land, price times quantity of product, and price times quantity of money. This process was dynamic. With the exception of the quantity of land—each specific plot of land and presumably its fertility—all the other factors were changing over time. Over time the price of the land went down, *because*—clearly—the cumulative quantity of fruit to be derived from the purchased plot of land went progressively down to zero as the 49th year approached, the year of the restitution of the land. This sliding scale method for calculating the price of the land at any given moment is evident: there was less fruit to be gathered as time progressed. Yet, what is not evident is that the economic system relied on two hidden independent relationships: the price of the fruit of the land and the value (quantity times price) of money. These relationships have to be made explicit:

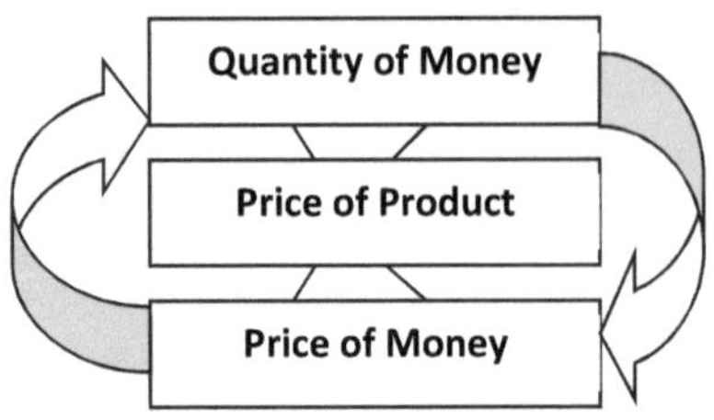

Figure 2. The Monetary Mechanism

The unit price of the fruit of the land had to remain *constant* over time; and the value of money also had to remain *constant* over time—otherwise, it would have been impossible to determine the price of a plot of land at any point in time. To wit, if the price of the fruit were to increase over time, then the price of the land could either remain constant—rather than decrease—or even increase over time. Ditto for any variation in the value of money.

We shall investigate the issue of the value of money after analyzing the legal and moral context in which the Jubilee was carried out. Here it might be worth to remain a little longer on the issue of the constancy of the price of the fruit of the land. Assume zero initial capital expenditure, constant labor costs, and no technological innovation over time, the cost of the product ought to remain *constant*. (Indeed, with technological innovation, as current market trends in computers demonstrate, in a regimen of near perfect competition the price of a product will decrease).

The Legal Context. The legal operative word is stewardship. As distinguished from "things" that we create and on which we have legitimate property rights, the land belongs neither to its possessor, nor to the government. The owner of the land is Yahweh. "The land is mine," says Yahweh (Lev 25:23). It is Yahweh who gives the land to each family of the tribes of Israel—except the Levi (Num 18:20) who were expected to live on part of the tithe (Num 18:24-30; cf. Kelly 2004). If one possessor encounters troubled economic waters, one can sell the fruit of the land. But the owner of the land remains Yahweh. And the price of the land goes down because at the Jubilee year the land goes back to the original possessor. Thus, the decreasing price makes it possible for the buyer to receive a compensation equivalent to the value of product that might be obtained until the 49th year of the Jubilee cycle. And, incidentally, it is worth noticing that it becomes less traumatic and more palatable to transfer back to the original possessor a plot of land whose residual market value goes down to zero—instead of remaining constant or increasing—as the Jubilee year approaches. (Urban houses are treated like consumer goods. They are not returned to the original owner, specifies Myron S. Geller, unless redeemed.)

The Moral Context. In Israel there was a moral obligation to return the land to the original possessor at the Jubilee year. Why this command? Why the acceptance of this command by the people—at least in the beginning? The reason is clear. The person without access to land and natural resources is not a free man or woman. This person has lost the most fundamental of God's gifts to man; he has lost his freedom. The loop is closed, the inner mechanism of the economics of Moses becomes clear as soon as it is realized—to repeat, as modern economic theory from Adam Smith onward has made clear—that freedom is an essential component of economic growth. No freedom, no wealth. Take away economic freedom from your neighbor and both you and your neighbor become poorer. Your nation becomes poorer. Thus the practice of the Jubilee concerning land does not only have internal legal and moral integrity, it makes unexceptionable and irreproachable economic sense. [Especially in olden days, access to land was an essential component of economic freedom. Concentration of the land in a few hands restricts the economic freedom existing in a nation. The injunction of the Jubilee concerning land is an essential tool of an economic policy that wants to prevent hoarding and to preserve economic freedom for the nation as a whole.] Let us now observe the inner mechanism of the Jubilee concerning money. Similarities and differences with the theory and practice of the Jubilee concerning land are quite instructive. Naturally, one reinforces the other.

Jubilee Concerning Money

The second plank of the Jubilee is the injunction that during the seventh year all personal debts (only) among the Hebrews are to be extinguished. This injunction—if ever practiced, especially outside of kinship, specifies Myron Geller—can be understood when it is inserted into a monetary framework that is dominated by these three fundamental propositions: Gold, or an equivalent commodity, is money. Debt is not money. Interest rate is zero or very near zero. To analyze these propositions, let us reconstruct the monetary framework which led the Israelites to their unique injunction. Three elements are in proportional relationship:

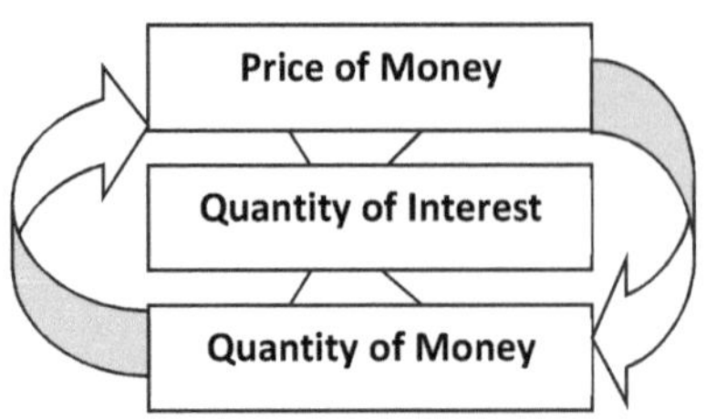

Figure 3. A Monetary Framework

In the beginning the supply of gold, being a global commodity, increased—though in spurts—at a near constant rate with the increase of the population. Hence, since its per capita utility was rather constant, the price of money was stable. The interest rate was zero (Lev 25:36-37) because the gold nugget or coin that was returned was the same as—or an equivalent to—the one borrowed; in this case the value implicit in the use of the nugget was a definite gift from the lender to the borrower. (*In the beginning,* unless other arrangements were instituted, in order to avoid paying or receiving a 100% interest rate in addition to the return of the capital, one would have had to break apart the nugget or the coin—a difficulty that was eventually obviated by issuing coins of smaller and smaller denominations. And if in time a reasonable interest rate was charged, one still remained within the bounds of the economics of the Jubilee.) *In the beginning,* money as debt did not exist. The relation between debtor and creditor remained personal and static. One did not buy or sell debt. Who would want to buy an "asset"—debt—that bears low or no interest and whose value becomes zero when the Jubilee year comes due?

But why did the value of debt become zero when the seventh year arrived? The practical reason is that the borrower had almost certainly spent the nugget or the coin borrowed and was now penniless: personal peonage did exist, but was subject to the same rules as those concerning monetary debt (see Lev 25:39-55). The cancellation of debt and the redemption from peonage renders men free again—and free human beings produce more than slaves and peons. The theoretical reason is that the cancellation of debt on the seventh year was the capstone that held an extremely delicate set of checks and balances together: the interest rate was null or very low and certainly there was no such construct as compound interest; debt had no value of its own; indeed, gold used as cash had—literally—a carrying cost and was not much subject to inflation or deflation. These relationships persisted as long as the Jubilee and Sabbatical were practiced.

Apart from the internal coherence of the system, where is the fundamental justification for the cancellation of debts during the seventh year? The case of land is clear. Yahweh creates the land; therefore, Yahweh remains its owner in perpetuity. But who creates money? Unless other textual evidence is brought forward, there is only one expression that clarifies the issue. The expression comes from Lk 20:24-25, in which Jesus, upon being shown a denarius, asked: "Whose portrait and inscription are on it?" "Caesar's," they replied. He said to them, "Then give to Caesar what is Caesar's". This is who Jesus understood to be the intermediate owner of money: Caesar; the government.

But wait. Who is the King in the Jewish tradition? What is the government? The King is anointed by Yahweh. The King and the government are representatives of Yahweh. The money, then, is as much a good that comes from Yahweh as the land. (And this, incidentally, is the foundational reason for the institution of the tithe [see Gn 14:20; Lev 27:30; and Deut 14:22]. The tithe is similar to the first fruit that in Greece or Rome and other ancient societies, and in Bali today, is given to the gods).

Thus the Jubilee/Sabbatical concerning money, the remission of all debts every seventh year, makes as much sense as the restitution of the land to the original possessor. This injunction of the Jubilee concerning money possesses just as much internal logic, as well as legal and moral integrity, as the Jubilee concerning land. The unexceptionable and irreproachable economic sense of the Jubilee concerning the land is redoubled when it assumes the form of the cancellation of debts—the cancellation of the duty to restitute wealth that no longer is there. Yet, to make the issues more deeply understood, perhaps one must ask: what is money?

Money. There is no definition of money in economic theory. And there can be none. In economic theory, there is only an explanation of the functions of money: a store of value, a means of exchange, and a tool of accounting. These, to repeat, are the functions of money. For a definition of money, one must go to the law. One can then say with certainty what money is: Money is a contract. Money is a contract between the holder of the coin—or the note—and society. It is society as a whole that gives value to the money. It is the sweat and tears of all the people that give value to money. The King, or the government, as representative of society as a whole, only vouches for its mint condition and guarantees the value of money.

Both money and land are common goods, because they are both given value by the sweat and tears of all the people in the land. A rock in Arizona is nearly worthless;

a rock of the same size in Manhattan is worth gazillions. To repeat, the Jubilee does not only have internal logical, legal, and moral integrity, it makes unexceptionable and irreproachable economic sense. The practice of cancellation of debt every seventh year was an acceptance of reality and an institution of peace: one cannot spill blood from a stone. The alternative is to enslave debtors. Yet, debtors produce nothing if incarcerated—indeed, they cost money for sustenance—and slaves produce less than free men. Hence, society as a whole, just as in the case of the land, is worse off through the pursuance of sleek economic practices. These practices are generally tolerated because the cost of the sustenance of the debtor in jail is borne, not by the creditor, but by society as a whole.

This analysis is confirmed by a view of the monetary system as a whole. The monetary system has to integrate three elements: (1) a coin or a bill is to be made equivalent to (2) a unit of currency—e.g., one dollar bill; and both have to be made equivalent to (3) some amount of real wealth. This third element is shattered into an infinite number of items. The functionality of the system is ultimately determined by the (culturally always changing) exchange values among these infinite sets: one ounce of gold for one bushel of apples, and one bushel of apples for a carved walking stick, which at that one point in time must in turn be able to buy an ounce of gold. In a free economy, these exchange values are determined by the laws of supply and demand. Yet, this conclusion is much too hurried, because these exchange values are *first* determined by the number and the value of bills and coins in circulation. In other words, two thirds of monetary analysis consists of the determination of who issues the currency, conditions of issuance, and amount of currency in circulation. If the amount of currency determines the nominal value of the currency, then the essence of monetary *policy* consists of the determination of elements (1) and (2) above, namely who issues the currency and to whom is it issued—and, more specifically, the conditions under which the currency is created. To confine one's observation to the third element of the monetary process is not wrong; it is an incomplete action. It is condemning oneself to a partial view of the process: It is as if, while diligently studying all twirls, all twists and turns, of the cat, one lost track of the cat. Worse. This is not simply a theoretical conclusion. To study only the third element of the monetary process, it is not simply to abandon monetary policy to the blind forces of the market. This enclosure of vision inexorably leads to the abandonment of monetary policy either to the bankers or the politicians.

Clearly, in a duly constituted society it is not the creditor who creates the currency or its value, but the monetary authority in conjunction with the actions of the free market. The monetary authority is thus fully entitled to cancel uncollectible debts. Money is fiat money. It should not be made into a means of control over people. The monetary aspects of the Jubilee are, therefore, in full accord with a complete understanding of the monetary system as a whole.

Jubilee Concerning Products-Things-Time

One meaning of Jubilee is not just restitution, but gift. There are many sides to these injunctions: one is economic, the others are legal, social, moral, and religious; today we might add one more dimension: psychological. The Israelites are enjoined to offer gifts to the passerby, the sojourner, and the poor. A list of injunctions runs as follows: at all times, leave the corn stalk at the edge of the field untouched; leave the fruit on the lower branches of the tree untouched; leave whatever stock of grain falls from your cart so that any passerby can avail himself of this bounty—no questions asked. This proviso is all important. Its importance is made manifest not so much by the intrusive questioning of the "welfare state" of today as by the extraordinary delicacy of moral sentiments epitomized by Maimonides, the Jewish sage of the XII century Spain in which the three monotheistic religions working together, not without shortcomings, created a splendid civilization. The practice of charity—the *tzedakah*—is codified in Maimonides' "golden ladder", in which (as in the Islamic practice of *zakāh*) ultimately the line between morality and economics is overstepped and the wisdom to endow people with a business of their own is established. Why, one might ask? Because Maimonides and traditional Islamic jurists can be said to have discovered that competition is the soul of economic freedom.

The practical effects of these injunctions are multifaceted. Each injunction orders a transfer of wealth from a producer to a consumer—without any compensation, because, presumably, the passerby who avails himself of that bounty has no means to compensate the producer. The economic effect of this aspect of the Jubilee is straightforward. Consumption, as Adam Smith well knew, is "the sole end and purpose" of business: consumption completes the economic process. A penny is earned when a good is sold. If you cannot sell a product, first reduce its price—or make more money available to the consumer, as Henry Ford well knew—and then give it away This economic aspect of the Jubilee, liberally extended to cover the Sabbatical and everyday practices, should be most evident today. What board of directors will order an expansion of business when merchandise is stuck on the shelves?

The social/religious/moral/psychological effect of this aspect of the Jubilee resides in the meaning of Jubilee as freedom: freedom from attachment to products, attachment to things— which we create and on which we have proper property rights. And to the list of attachments, today, one must add time. We are so attached to our freedom to do whatever we please with our time that we neglect to offer it, at least every seventh day, to our families and our communities—and ultimately to ourselves and preferably to God. How can the wisdom of the practice of the Sabbath have slid from our hands so irresponsibly? Perhaps it will help us to understand, if we decipher Pharaoh's message contained in Ex 5:9 along such explicit lines as: "Let us so overwork the people that they will be incapable of listening to words of truth". And of course the core of the Jewish message is that Yahweh grants us freedom to worship him without fear all the days of our life—a freedom that clearly extends to the choice not to worship him.

[The guess is that we have not considered the many implications of free time. Perhaps it will help us to understand, if we decipher Pharaoh's message contained in Ex 5:9 along such explicit lines as: "Let us so overwork the people that they will be incapable of listening to words of truth." Perhaps it will help us to understand the need to abstain from work on the Sabbath day, if we consider the relationships between free time and all the work that needs to be done in order to insure one's economic freedom: One needs to insure the health of one's own physical body; one needs to insure the health of political body of the nation. One needs to think. One needs to have the time to get out of one's own limited shell. And of course the core of the Jewish message is that Yahweh grants us freedom to worship him without fear all the days of our life—a freedom that clearly extends to the choice not to worship him.]

Only a saint could have understood the deepest possible aspects of the detachment from products, things, and even time. Saint Catherine of Siena says (1980, p. 322): "(Those who are detached from things) do not fear the bitterness of death." The right relation with products, things, and time grants the greatest freedom of all: freedom from fear of dying—a fear experienced a thousand times by many a person who is abnormally attached to things. If in doubt, Google "hoarding" and be amazed at the findings.

Seen in the total complexity of the economic aspects of the Jubilee, the second doctrine of the economics of Moses—a well-known doctrine—ought to acquire its original full force: *Do Not Steal*. Do not steal money and do not steal land, it is clear, because they do not belong to you, or even to their possessors. They are common goods. Ultimately they both belong to Yahweh. If you steal land or money, you offend Yahweh—directly.

The injunction against stealing extends to consumer goods as well. And here the legal and moral foundation of the injunction is as strong as it can possibly be. In a primitive society, there is no mystery as to the origin of consumer goods. They issue directly from the sweat and tears of people. Hence, these goods belong to those who have created them. More. In a primitive society in which consumer goods are not only few but essential to life, stealing them is tantamount to killing other people.

Does one dare ask the quintessential moral-practical question: Is it all any different today? Are there not people starving—even starving to death—today?

This, of course, is a paper devoted to economics. Where is the economic rationale for the injunction against stealing? The forms of stealing are legion; and so are the costs of stealing. Unjustly dispossessed people are less productive than people who are secure in their possessions. Indeed, stealing is the ultimate form of corruption. Economics is just beginning to appreciate the costs of corruption in the business world—both within developed and developing countries. Would any financial crisis be as severe, if there were no corruption in high places?

***

A Preliminary Evaluation. The extremely delicate sets of checks and balances composing the economics of Moses doomed it to a relatively short life. As soon as either greed became unbridled or the theological bonds were loosened, the system could no longer work. But while it worked, what a system it was; what a beacon to the ages. It was the creation of a perfectly just economy. Israel must have indeed been so rich as to attract the envy of its neighbors, even so often to become the object of conquest and plunder

A Question. People ask: Was the Jubilee really practiced? An imprecise answer is that the Jubilee was practiced with a decreasing intensity from—before?—the time of Moses to the time of Jesus, and that the legal mantel of stewardship covering land and money worked, and worked quite well for society as a whole. Hence, a more precise answer: The Jubilee was practiced as long as the people of Israel remained free. And that is the rub! The absence of chicanery and theft coupled with the practice of the Jubilee, the return of the land to the original possessors and the cancellation of debts after so many years, restored the inner balance of the economic relationships in Israel. There were no poor (Deut 15:4), or very few poor people. Investment occurred naturally—so much so that Moses did not need to speak of investment.

Would the Economics of Moses Have Been Practiced in a Non-Theocratic Society? The answer is an undiluted, Yes. The economics of Moses has been practiced since time immemorial, and still is being practiced: in the commons, until they are enclosed. (A WORTHY PAUSE. *Private ownership tends to be absolute. It wants to enclose the commons, against the Bible's injunction never to sell the commons [Lev 25:34]; even at the cost of the demise of the enclosed commons—as Hardin well knew. This is the chain reaction: monetization of the enclosures leads to overcapitalization because initial expenditures of money must be recovered at a profit and on time; overcapitalization leads to overexploitation and speculation, which lead to financial and natural collapse. There has never been a collapse of the commons; there has always and everywhere been a collapse of the enclosures.*) The size of the economy is not the issue, either. The economics of Moses was practiced by the American Indians over the vast prairies when they were free.

The substance of the economics of Moses can be summarized simply. Morality creates freedom; and freedom creates wealth. The freedom of wealth acquired in justice ultimately produces jubilation in the heart. That is the ultimate aim of the economics of Moses.

Now is the time to go from the economics of Moses to the economics of Jesus in order to discern more clearly the relationship between economic freedom and investment.

Three doctrines comprise the economics of Jesus: *Invest Your Talents; Do Not Hoard Your Talents; Give to Caesar What Is Caesar's.*

1. Invest Your Talents

From Moses to Jesus Investing as the Normal Outcome of Economic Freedom

The word "investment" had not been invented yet, but the practice was there from time immemorial—if not from the first appearance of men and women on earth. And so was the intellectual understanding that this practice revolves around three factors of production: land, capital, and labor. We have observed how Israel intellectually handled both money and land from Moses to Jesus. Why is labor not an essential component of the economics of Moses?

In the beginning there was work, but no "labor." Every member of the tribes of Israel received a plot of land for his own use, except the Levi who were to live on 1/10 of the tithe. Therefore, **everyone was an owner**, *not a worker or a laborer*—and the practice of the Jubilee tended to reinforce this status. Hence there was economic freedom in the land. From Moses to Jesus investing was such a normal outcome of economic freedom that Moses did not have to speak of investing at all. By the time of Jesus, evidently much economic freedom had already been eroded. The Jubilee was no longer practiced. Indeed, with the Roman conquest the Mosaic mantel of stewardship over land and money was captured by the Roman institution of private property. Acquisition was in the saddle. Most people lost possession of their land and debts impoverished them even faster. Some people became laborers. Jesus has a forceful account of the condition of labor. Mt 20:8-15 gives this parable of the workers in the vineyard who at the end of the day …lined up to receive their pay. The ones hired last were paid first. Having worked but an hour, they didn't expect much. To their surprise and delight, however, they each received a full denarius. When the workers who were hired first saw this, they—forgetting their bargain— became happily expectant. If that was what the employer was paying to those who had worked but a single hour, then how much more would they have coming! So they thought. When they received their own pay, however, it was but one denarius, like the others. Their fallen expectation turned to bitterness, and they confronted the employer, saying: "These last have wrought but one hour, yet thou hast made them equal to us, who have bourne the burden and the heat of the entire day." The employer, however, was not impressed. To one of them, he replied: "Friend, I am not being unfair to you. Didn't you agree to work for a denarius? Take your pay and go. I want to give this man who was hired last the same as I gave you. Don't I have the right to do what I want with my own money? Or are you envious because I am generous?"

As all parables, this too has received a myriad of interpretations. The present context suggests this meaning. This is what Jesus seems to say: "Yahweh gave you possession of the land; Moses gave you the Jubilee to correct your possible economic mistakes. If you tolerate a system in which there is no Jubilee or any of its equivalents, you have no economic freedom. You have a system of masters and slaves. And, legally as well as theologically, you cannot tell the master what to do. You can cry to high haven, but not even God is going to listen to you. Either you regain your God-given economic freedom, whereby you yourself (in concord with other co-owners if you have any) have the right to reward your endeavors in accordance with what you think is just, or you simply have to accept what the master decides to give you—no matter how arbitrary; no matter how unjust; no matter, even, how generous that reward is."

This is the condition that still prevails. That is why, for instance, all attempts to establish a "living wage" are destined to fail—no matter how well-intentioned, no matter how persistently pursued. Outside the institution of ownership of land, of capital, and of one's own labor, there is no way of accounting what is just or unjust— or even logical. As Franco Modigliani (1980, p. xiv) frankly admitted, there is "no rigorous analysis" of "the mechanism determining wages and prices…. Indeed, the modeling of wage behavior remains to this day the Achilles heel of macroeconomic analysis." The shortcut is, and will forever be, to treat labor as a commodity.

Are we left by Jesus forever without recourse against intrinsic injustices of the "wage contract? Not at all. As Jesus implied, to redress injustices, the labor movement has to transform itself into the ownership or equity movement—with union dues attached, not to wages, but to ownership shares. The list of inalienable rights of workers will never become full enough to yield a satisfactory solution to the "labor question"; this list must be transformed into a single item: the right to own the fruits created by one's labor—a right that has to cover capital appreciation.

Jesus thus emphasizes what Moses implied and what every Classical economist was later (almost) to emphasize: Take proper care of (the ownership of) land, capital, and labor and economic growth will result as a normal outcome of economic freedom. Yet, were we to leave the issue at that we would be making a grievous mistake. We would be neglecting the historical context and, consequently, we would not foster a true understanding of the economics of Jesus.

From Moses to Adam Smith Investing Is Done in Accordance with the Moral Law

 As there are many planks in the economics of Moses that need to be made explicit, so there is one essential corollary of the doctrine of Jesus regarding investment that must be brought forward: From Moses to Adam Smith, everyone agreed that economic life is covered by the moral law. The understanding of this complex interlacing of moral and economic injunctions was held astonishingly constant over time. This view, confirms Wood (2002, p. 83), was "the same as Aristotle's". It is only from Adam Smith onward that there has been a breach in this tradition. (Free marketers assume that this reality still prevails—and, in a fundamental way, they are right.)

Modern economics, it is widely maintained, is a science—indeed, a mathematical and an autonomous science. As such, economics is supposed to be studied by itself and, certainly, its internal cohesion precludes the examination of any external consideration; especially any consideration regarding morality. These statements, by themselves, are inarguable. Yet, as most people sense, they are fallacious. Their fallacy is revealed only realizing that they do not stand alone but are part of an intellectual system whose fundamental propositions are as follows:

1. Freedom $\rightarrow \infty$
2. Morality $\rightarrow 0$
3. (Monetary) Efficiency $= 1$ (sole value)
4. Economic agents $= ||$ (isolated logical automatons)
5. Community $\rightarrow 0$.

In Appendix A we shall demonstrate that not one of these propositions stands at the touch of reason. For the time being, suffice to notice that the conflict between morality and economics is not a postulate of modern economics; the moral consequences of economics are immaterial to economists. Therefore, the separation of morality from economics can be considered as a transient phenomenon, a transient aberration that time will allow us to forget. We will then discover that Adam's Fallacy (Foley 2006), with all its rationalizations, has gone away by blinking it away. Here we can only distil the extended analysis into the following proposition: Human beings are free—not to choose between Gucci and Pucci—but between good and evil.

Let us parse this sentence. Economic growth is not a monotonic function of freedom. There are two forces that move human life and, by definition, the economic system: one is freedom, the other is morality. Jesus was very specific as to what he meant by morality. He did not fall into the trap of determining for others what is good or evil. Jesus did not make this severe strategic error. As outstanding proofs, he did not suggest any external restriction on economic activity or any forcible transfer of wealth from one group of people to another. Hence, he would concur that economic activity must be free and he would add that morality cannot be imposed—or slapped on—from the outside, because then morality becomes empty of content. Either morality is within each and every decision that one takes or it is not there at all. Thus Jesus made it very clear that he wanted morality to be applied ever creatively. He wanted moral rules to be forever internalized. And easily memorized. He reduced the whole of morality in economics to two economic doctrines: *Do not Hoard; Give to Caesar What Is Caesar's.*

2. Do Not Hoard

The freedom to choose between Gucci and Pucci is not an economic decision. It is an esthetic decision. The economic decision is whether to spend one's income and wealth on consumer and capital goods or to hoard it. Analysis shows that this choice is more than a simple economic decision; it is an intrinsically moral decision with clearly identifiable economic consequences. Jesus was extraordinarily firm about this choice, which—since reasonable people are assumed to buy consumer goods only as they need them and moral people are supposed to know how to choose between buying *another* Gucci bag or giving the money to the neighbor who is starving—he characteristically reduced it to the choice between investing and hoarding. In the Parable of the Talents as written in Mt 25:14-30, Jesus so forcefully applauded using wealth creatively that all the wealth was donated to those who had doubled it—and they were enthusiastically entrusted with the administration of much more wealth. Clearly, Jesus applauded investing so because moral people are supposed to know the difference between producing a Gucci bag or a loaf of bread. By the same token, Jesus so strongly condemned hoarding as to take the one talent away from the person who, for fear of losing it, planted it underground where it could do no good for anyone. Much more. This person was ordered to be cast into hell, literally "the outer darkness; (w)here men will weep and gnash their teeth". No appeal. No mercy.

Only understanding the economic consequences of hoarding does one see that Jesus was fully justified in such an uncharacteristically strong and uncharitable position. Those who doubt the relevance of hoarding in relation to the modern economy might want to read Appendix B first. Or they might want to fast forward (which in actual time is fast backward) to reading *The Economic Process.* There they will discover that hoarding is the hidden-to-economists bottleneck that strangles economic growth (235-70); that hoarding is the hidden-to-economists seed of inflation (271-302); that hoarding has the hidden-to-economists property of being in a one-to-one relationship with the level of poverty (329-53). Without the need for too much elaboration, readers will also discover that, through the transmission belt of economic rights and responsibilities, the elimination of hoarding is ultimately the spring of Economic Liberty, Economic Freedom and Economic Justice for all (355-58).

Should anyone wonder that Jesus was such a superb economist and political scientist? Well, those who might want to confine Jesus to the straightjacket of theology, will have to admit that Jesus' doctrine of not hoarding becomes clearer if, first and foremost, it is seen as an explicit formulation—and an extension—of the clear and compelling Mosaic Law of the Jubilee, the clear-as-a-bell and compelling-as-a-knocker Mosaic Law of the Jubilee.

Do Not Hoard in the Mosaic Law

As expressed in the Jewish Law, the injunction against hoarding is presented as a list of positive activities, which in a decreasing order of importance can be enumerated as follows: return the land to the original possessor every forty-nine years; cancel all existing debts every seven years; let the land lie fallow every seven years; reserve the Sabbath, the seventh day of the week, for God and community, for family, and for yourself; leave the corn stalk at the hedge of the field untouched; leave the fruit on the lower branches of the tree untouched; leave whatever stock of grain falls from your cart so that any passerby can avail himself of this bounty—no questions asked, no compensation required.

Jesus synthesized the list of positive actions prescribed by the Mosaic law and the Jewish prophets into a negative injunction: do not hoard. Thus he generalized and extended the original formulation of this injunction, by including in it all forms of hoarding. This formulation has a set of explicatory characteristics of its own. In it, the economic—as distinguished from the theocratic and moral—aspects of the Jubilee become exceedingly transparent. The fundamental reason why at the appointed years the land had to be returned to the original tiller and debts had to be cancelled was to prevent hoarding: the inordinate accumulation of wealth in the hands of the few—and the consequent deprivation for the many of the means of sustenance. With the amount of wealth being finite at any particular moment, when the few have too much, the many have too little. (Technically, wealth hoarded is only wealth that is used neither as a consumer good nor as a capital good. The land ordered back to the original possessor might not have all been hoarded. Yet, most of it was—as the existence of much unused land indicated.) The Prophet Mohammed put it most simply and clearly: "Let him who owns land cultivate it himself, and if he does not do so let him have his brother cultivate it" (Chapra, 1985, p. 85). The Arapaho American Indians put this commandment this way: "Take only what you need and leave the land as you found it" (Zona, 1994, p. 88).

Jesus was very clear as to this relationship. For him cause and effect was so immediate that he emphasized in no uncertain terms the destination of the wealth not to be hoarded: It ought to be given to the poor. He felt so strongly about the issue that he personalized it. He said in Mt 25:40: "whatever you did for one of the least of these brothers of mine, you did for me."

Why did Jesus emphasize so forcefully the need of giving to the poor? Generally, this injunction is characterized as being a moral injunction. And that is certainly true; but it is not a sufficient interpretation of Jesus' position. It is the economic content of this injunction that links the economics of Moses to the economics of Jesus and gives substance to the moral injunction of giving to the poor: giving to the poor not just a pittance, but giving them what is their due. We have so far seen that the Israelites—let alone the rest of the world—by not practicing any of the forms of the Jubilee had gradually lost their original economic freedom. And the number of poor people was growing at an intolerable pace. Certainly, there were many more poor people at the time of Jesus than at the time of Moses. But this is a historical fact that does not explain much; indeed, it is a trend that needs to be explained. A major institutional change occurred from the time of Moses to the time of Jesus. Hebrew stewardship of land and money was transformed into Roman private ownership of land and money: land and money were privatized. These common goods could then be accumulated beyond the requirement of the satisfaction of one's needs. The latifundia—those exceedingly large estates that still plague the world today—were born; and the insidious accumulation of financial resources was beginning to be felt in the economic system. A part of these resources was accumulated and kept idle—all the while people were excluded from their utilization and were made poor as a consequence. With the latifundia came poverty.

This, then, is the first essential characteristics of Jesus' doctrine of not hoarding. By turning his own negative into a positive injunction, the doctrine acquires an economic content that does not stand in a vacuum but is immediately related to the rest of society. The poor are poor not because the rich are rich nor because the rich are the creators of poverty (cf. Gorga, 1998)—Jesus had nothing against the rich. The poor are poor because the rich have too much, too much they do not need. The second essential characteristic of Jesus' doctrine of not hoarding is this. It places the primary responsibility for not hoarding, implicitly on society and the law, but explicitly on individual conscience. Hoarding clearly becomes a moral issue with distinct economic consequences. Dishoarding becomes a voluntary act. Jesus wanted each one of us to be convinced of the importance of our own rights and responsibilities and to act upon them. Jesus did not start an economic movement. The third essential characteristic of Jesus' doctrine of not hoarding is this: Do not wait forty-nine years before divesting yourself of unneeded wealth. The time to dishoard is now. And with this he exalted the value of practices recommended in Mosaic and rabbinic law.

Hoarding from Jesus to Locke

It seems that from Jesus to Locke (1698, esp. Bk. II, Ch. V, pars. 46-51) everyone knew about hoarding and the need to give to the poor. St. John Chrysostom (347-407), concerned with how to give to the poor, exploded (Tierney, 1959, p. 55): "Let us have no more of this ridiculous, diabolical, peremptory prying" into the lives of people who ask for assistance. With various dissenting opinions, the Catholic Church from its beginning up until the age of Adam Smith maintained that surplus wealth of the rich legally belonged to the poor (*ibid.* esp. pp. 22-44).

Thus the moral injunction of giving to the poor was transformed into a strict—however imperfectly practiced—legal injunction: the surplus of one's wealth, whatever one—on the basis of one's own independent counsel—did not need, belonged do the poor (*ibid.* esp. p. 106). The poor took the place of the original owner of the Jewish Law of the Jubilee. The penalty was excommunication. The same was true in relation to usury, which in its simplest formulation can be defined as the request of exorbitant rates of interest. Usury, the fastest method for people to grow rich at the expense of others who need to borrow money, was consistently discouraged from Jesus to Locke.

Islamic law against usury is the only stronghold left against hoarding in the modern world and it has given rise to innovative practices that range from microfinancing to equity-financing.

Why? Why this disappearance of the concern for hoarding in the modern world? The answer to this puzzle is extraordinarily simple. The disappearance of the concern for hoarding has occurred because the practice of hoarding goes undetected in modern economic theory.

The Disappearance of Hoarding in Modern Economic Theory Since Adam Smith

Enter Adam Smith into the field of economics and the memory of three thousand years of history is erased from our consciousness. Hoarding disappears from sight. Not for naught Adam Smith is considered the father of modern economics. Today, economists can no longer see hoarding. Economists may even talk about hoarding, but formally—mathematically and logically—hoarding, as is well known, cannot enter into even the most minute interstices of modern economic theory. All income that is not spent on consumer goods is assumed to be saved and all saving is assumed to be "equal" to investment: there is no room for hoarding. Hoarding disappeared from the purview of economic theory when Adam Smith, being no economist but a professor of moral philosophy, unawares conflated two conflicting categories of thought, two irreconcilable phenomena—hoarding and investment (capital)—into one: accumulation. Worse still. Adam Smith saw a distinction between saving and investment (1776, Bk. II., Ch. 3, pars. 14-18) that, since it is nowhere to be found in economic reality, has in vain been searched for in economic theory. Not for naught the relationship between saving and investment is officially classified as a quagmire. In fact, the distinction between saving and investment is only a differentiation between two degrees of risk—hence, two different degrees of potential income stream. There is no conceptual, no purely economic distinction between saving and investment.

Damn the reality. Damn sound economic reasoning. Damn economic theory. Full speed ahead. When Adam Smith entered the field of economics, saving took the place of hoarding. Hoarding was relegated to the past (1776, Bk. V., Ch. 3, pars. 1, 2, 9) and disappeared from sight.

Worse, much worse things were to follow. Since he had no understanding of the morality of economics and—pity for a professor of moral philosophy (and a deist)— he had an ax to grind against the morality of the monks (see esp. 1776, B. V. Ch. 1, par. 158), Adam Smith preached the doctrine of "accumulation of riches" (see esp. 1776, B. II, Ch. 3, par. 35).

At that moment, losing its moorings in morality, economics lost its rudder and sense of direction. It became a mechanistic discipline. Under the guidance of modern economic theory, the economic system is assumed to be ruled, not by human decisions, but by "the blind forces of the market." Man is out of the saddle. Man is assumed to be an innocent bystander.

A Modern Chorus of Approval

Having lost the memory of the past, most economists stand ready to proclaim the inevitability of the present. At this juncture in the conversation, joining their voices to a chorus of free-marketers (who assume that morality is practiced, as it is practiced, by all self-respecting economic agents) and winner-take-all analysts who study the economics of gambling and Hollywood stardom, most economists are likely to pitch in and say: "The forces of the market, rather than justifying the economics of Moses and Jesus, prove that wealth accumulation—which is not recognized as being, in part, hoarding—is 'natural' and 'inevitable'. After all, did not Jesus, in Mt 26:11, quoting Deut 15:11, say, 'The poor will always be with you'"? These analysts have not factored in their analysis the distinction between hoarding ex post and hoarding ex ante. In so doing, they let the mechanics of hoarding pass under their radar undetected. Jesus was concerned with both stages of hoarding. He did not only say "Do Not Hoard" and, if you happened to have hoarded in the past, "Dishoard Now". Perhaps he was even more concerned with preventing hoarding from happening at all. He went after hoarding at its roots. He also said: "Give to Caesar What Is Caesar's." The evidence is strong that inordinate accumulation of wealth is due to the contravention of this last doctrine.

3. Give to Caesar What Is Caesar's

The third economic doctrine of Jesus, *Give to Caesar What Is Caesar's*, has traditionally been interpreted too narrowly. Betraying their intellectual roots in the work of Consultant Administrators from the fifteenth century Italy, modern economists have limited the application of this doctrine to the relationship between government and the governed. Thus, having abandoned monetary policy into the hands of the bankers, modern economists have not only reduced economic policy to fiscalism; more seriously still, they have restricted the vision of the economics of Jesus to a master/servant relationship. To understand the full import of the third economic doctrine of Jesus, we need to enlarge its range of applicability by enveloping the entire gamut of relations that exist among free men and women. Once one observes the whole economic process, as Classical economists did and as Keynes or Hayek did, then the third economic doctrine of Jesus reveals its not surprising complexity. The third doctrine then reads as follows: give the other fellow what is his due. This, as it has been known from Aristotle onward, is the very essence of economic justice. Once that is done, we shall see that giving to Caesar what is Caesar's is nothing but the application of Moses Law: Do not steal. Jesus did not present any new proposition in Jewish Law. He simply transformed a negative Mosaic commandment, "Do not steal", into a positive injunction: "Do Justice". Thus he followed Deut 16:20.

Let us leave petty larceny well alone. To put substance into this third doctrine, let us realize that when people do not pay the full share of the taxes they owe, especially taxes on land and natural resources, they steal from fellow citizens who are burdened with the total share of the costs of running a country. When the central bank sells the national credit to preferred customers, the central bank sells for a mess of pottage a national treasure that belongs to the entire population. Private appropriation of common goods—such as land and money—without compensation is expropriation and plunder. When stockholders cash in the value of their stocks and bonds, they rob the workers who have originally contributed to the creation of that value—and are excluded from that bounty by the faulty legal institute of "wage contract". When one purchases a whole corporation, and uses other people's money to concentrate the wealth of the nation into fewer and fewer hands, one robs at least the workers, if not also the previous as well as future potential stockholders, of the ensuing capital appreciation of the corporation.

Set these four economic mechanisms of capital accumulation aright, and hoarding is cut at its root. You will Give to Caesar What Is Caesar's. You will do justice and receive justice. With a just distribution of wealth, there is no need for its redistribution. Indeed, you will implement the spirit of Moses' Jubilee. Clearly, Jesus not only explicitly called for the application of Moses' Jubilee (esp. Lk 4:16-32 read with the help of Trocmé 1973, pp. 26-29); to preserve their spirit, he changed the form of Moses' injunctions and adapted them to the needs of the moment.

Some Effects of the Economics of Moses and the Economics of Jesus

The economy that invests its talents; the economy that does not hoard; the economy that gives to each his due is a full participant in the economics of Moses and Jesus—a set of doctrines whose central tenets, a preliminary investigation reveals, are shared by virtually all religious systems. This is an economy in which agents are neither automatons nor abstractions, but fully integrated persons composed of body, mind, and soul (does one prefer "character" as the free integrative factor between mind and body?); men and women who—endowed with a full complement of virtues and vices—are confronting fundamental questions at every step in their journey, because economics is not the result of blind forces; the economic process is the result of simple and clear choices. This is an economy in which both secular and religious leaders feel the responsibility to suggest that men and women should follow the virtues rather than their vices—for their immediate and ultimate good, as well as for the good of everyone else. This is an economy in which costs are fully accounted for; real costs, not accounting fictions pursued through the subterfuge of externalities or by shifting costs of living onto the shoulders of the community. This is an economy in which the land, rather than being forced to produce more than it can, rather than being treated as a source of exploitation and a dumping ground, is treated as sacred. Hence the world is unencumbered of the threat of ecological disaster. This is an economy in which life is not reduced to money. This is an economy that exists in real time and produces real goods and services. In such an economy, efficiency cannot be separated from morality; rather, efficiency is a result of morality. This proposition bears repeating: Efficiency is the result of morality. This is an economy in which one does not only demand to receive economic justice at the hand of others; one extends economic justice to all others. This is an economy that runs to the tune of justice. This is an economy functioning within a just society.

The result of the economics of Moses and Jesus is peace and concord. Economics, properly professed, does not lead to strife; it is not made for man-wolf or for man-savage, as in the Hobbesian and Rousseauan abstractions, which lacked any understanding of economics and yet remain the dominating features in our spectrum of political considerations. Economics, properly professed, does not lead to begging, as we are all compelled to do these days. (Do not the rich beg for lower taxes? The middle classes for jobs? And the poor for entitlements?) The result of the economics of Moses and Jesus is not the frantic economy. The result of the economics of Moses and Jesus is serenity. And it is on the bedrock of serenity that a deep appreciation for life develops. Hence the economics of Moses, the economics of Jesus ultimately leads to the economics of jubilation—in the end, jubilation for the presence of Yahweh, giver of all the bounties of life. For Moses and Jesus, life is whole.

Where is the Evidence?

Where is the evidence, the reader might ask, that these are indeed the effects of the implementation of the economics of Moses and the economics of Jesus? The evidence lies in the economy of Zion in which the economics of Moses was implemented and in the economy of the Middle Ages in which the economics of Jesus was implemented. That Zion was the land of "milk and honey" (Ex 3:8) or that manna came down from heaven (Ex 16; Num 11:6-9; Ps 77:24-25; Wis 16:20) or that Moses struck the rock at Meriba twice to produce water—rather than simply praying for it, and was punished for his lack of faith—(Num 20:2-13) is not admissible evidence. Nor can one take historical accounts composed by Doctors of the Catholic Church as unbiased evidence. Reliable evidence, however, can be found elsewhere. The effects of the economics of Moses and the economics of Jesus have been studied by some of the most rabid adversaries of the Catholic Church; one might even call some of them enemies of Western civilization. These can be relied upon. Hence, for the effects of the implementation of the economics of Moses, the reader is invited to peruse the vast literature on the economy of the American Indians as they existed before the arrival of Columbus in Hispaniola, before Giovanni Caboto (an ancestor of the Cabots) reached the shores of New England, and before Sir Ferdinando Gorges (one of this writer's ancestors) became Proprietor of Maine. For the effects of the implementation of the economics of Jesus, the reader is invited to pore over paintings of Pieter Bruegel the Elder or Ambrogio Lorenzetti. The cultural background of Lorenzetti's *Allegory of Good Government* is not Judeo-

Christian but classical antiquity. For good measure, the fresco is located not in a church, but in Palazzo Pubblico (City Hall) of Siena.

A Personal Question and a Personal Answer

A personal question is often asked of a writer who writes along the lines written above: "Would you prefer to live in the economy of the Middle Ages?" A short personal answer is "No". A more extended one can be framed along these lines. No human institution is perfect. No period in history has been perfect. Nor will it ever be. The only issue is, can we do better today? If the response to this question is positive, then it behooves us to inquire how can we implement the tenets of the economics of Moses and the economics of Jesus in the full splendor and the full complexity of a modern economy. This is our next task, an essential task.

Part III — An Update

Within the economics of Moses and the economics of Jesus, wealth is not an end; wealth is a tool. Economics is not about money; economics is all about relationships among human beings. The goal of economics is not to become rich; it is to live— like human beings, in peace and justice, and in a state of jubilation. Modern economics, instead, seems to lead only to grumbling (cf. Ex 16:1-12). No matter how much we have, we never have enough. If the difference between modern economics and the economics of Moses and Jesus is so stark, is there any way of bridging the gap and investing our ancestral principles into the modern world? The economic Jubilee has not been practiced for millennia and, apart from the realm of Islamic law, policy restraints against hoarding have not been discussed, let alone practiced, for centuries. Is it even conceivable to insert the economics of Moses and Jesus into the modern world? The answer is rather simple and direct. To fit the economics of Moses and Jesus into the modern world, one must update economic theory; one must formulate a just economic policy; and one must start practicing what one preaches. We need to change, not our nature, but our social structures.

Updating Economic Theory

Contrary to likely expectations, it is modern economic theory that needs to be updated. Economic theory, as is widely recognized, is in a state of crisis. Indeed, it has been in a state of crisis at least since the publication in 1936 of Keynes' *General Theory*, the foundational work of modern economic theory. Following the recommendation of Keynes himself (1973, esp. pp. 47 and 150) or the recommendation of Friedrick Hayek ([1963]1995, p. 49 and 1994, p. 145), if one wants to solve the crisis in modern economic theory, one had better go back to the General Theory. And yet, once there, one is faced with a work that has often been described as wholly or in part "obscure" (see, e.g., Samuelson, 1946).

The reader will not be surprised to learn that the source of the deep avowed intellectual difficulties Keynes experienced in writing the General Theory (e.g., 1936, p. viii) resides in his unexamined acceptance of Adam Smith's conception of saving (Gorga 2002, pp. 79-92). In a hurry to solve the impossible intellectual problem of converting saving into investment, since saving is already an investment, by illegitimately equating the two Adam Smith spun the study of economics off a tangent into a world of shattered intellectualism in which, as Keynes (1936, p. 292) put it, "nothing is clear and everything is possible"; this is a world in which, as R. W. Goldsmith (1955-1956, p. 69n) calculated, saving assumes 100,000 logical meanings.

What is to be done? One needs to restrict the word saving to the world of finance. One then blinks away the silent revolution—the unheralded and undetected revolution—brought by Adam Smith to economics. By so doing, nothing is lost but confusion. All technical skills and all valid knowledge that have been acquired in the meantime are still there. Restoration can begin.
With room again available for the millennial conception of hoarding, formal changes in the General Theory (Gorga 2002, pp. 93-118, 139- 58) lead to this proposition: Investment = Income – Hoarding.

Three thousand years of history reappear to view. In fact, upon reflection, it can be seen that this statement contains nothing but the mathematical formulation of the Parable of the Talents. In this formulation is the seed of the mathematization of the economics of Jesus and the economics of Moses. The laborious logico-mathematical steps in this process (Gorga 2002, pp. 41-158) can be eschewed thanks to the assistance of geometry; only the results of these elaborations are given in Appendix C. The fundamental equation of the economics of Jesus can be represented by a Lorenz diagram in which Time is put on the horizontal axis and the Quantity of both investment (I) and hoarding (H) on the vertical axis:

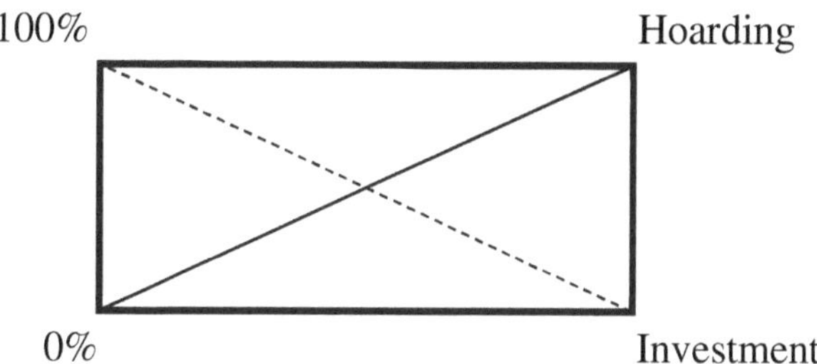

Figure 4. The Investment-Hoarding Nexus

Of course, this is a stylized representation of reality. Actual figures would produce much more erratic patterns, but the message is clear. At any one instant, the more investment, the less hoarding—and vice versa. The more real investment, the more growth of real goods and services. Hence, hoarding becomes visible as the determining factor of economic growth. This consequence is axiomatic. A little less evident is the discovery of the second major economic effect of hoarding: Hoarding is the determining factor of poverty. If, given appropriate economic policies, the more goods and services, the lower the levels of poverty in a nation; then, hoarding by the few creates artificial scarcity; it creates impossibility of investment by the many—and many fall so far behind as to become poor, to not be able to afford the basic necessities of life.

In figure 4, then, we find the essential elements of the aggregate supply function. As Brady (2004a, 2004b, and 2006) demonstrates, this function—and the aggregate demand function—is fully specified in the General Theory. The game "what Keynes really said" is over.

In our presentation, the aggregate demand function can be made visible by duplicating figure 4 and reading it solely in monetary terms. Through this process we basically separate the monetary economy from the real economy. Then, since there must be a relationship between these two components of the economic world, we search for a third element to link them together and we find it in the set of rules and regulations that in every society governs the distribution of ownership rights over real and monetary wealth—and we do not stray away from pure economic theory, because we are presented with the monetary value of those rights. Hence, we are given a new national accounting system. Analytical models—of stocks as well as flows—of real and monetary wealth can be found in Gorga (1982; 1991a; and 2002, pp. 25, 38, 156, 308-319).

Diagrammatically, this integration can be represented in this fashion:

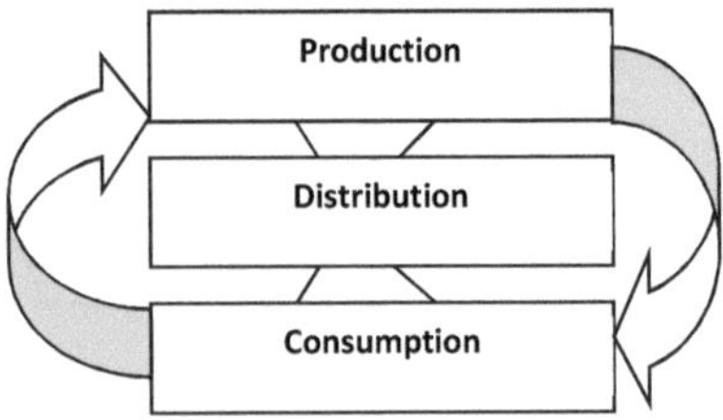

Figure 5. The Economic Process

Figure 5 reads as follows. When real goods and services pass from producers to consumers, monetary instruments of an equivalent value pass from consumers to producers. Then, one cycle of the economic process is completed—and is accompanied by the silent exchange of values of ownership rights over monetary and real wealth. Both money and goods change hands. The unit of account can be the economy of one person, one city, one nation, or the world as a whole. In macroeconomics, the exchange occurs neither between two insignificant commodities (cf. Schumpeter 1936) as in microeconomics nor between any two forms of financial instruments as in the economics of Wall Street. In macroeconomics, the total production of goods and services is exchanged for the total availability of financial resources—as in Keynes' principle of effective demand. The exchange of course occurs on the basis of relative prices as well as within the confines of a regimen of social and legal relationships, as best emphasized by the total opus of Friedrick Hayek.

One of the merits of figure 5 is that it describes the economic process as a whole. Everything is instantaneously related to everything else. Thus we bring the mathematics and geometry of economics up to the standards that prevail among engineers and scientists (see, e.g., Thompson 1986, p.36). We run away from the shattered world of the schools and go back to the world of Classical economists who knew that economics is composed of the integration of Production, Distribution, and Consumption of wealth. This integration can be made more specific by a more extensive reading of the terms, along these lines: Production is production of real goods and services (as studied especially by Supply-Side economists); Distribution is distribution of the value of ownership rights over real and monetary wealth (as studied especially by Institutionalists); Consumption is consumption—or expenditure—of monetary, i.e. financial instruments (as studied especially by Demand-Side economists).

Figure 5 depicts the economic process at one instant in time. The process over time is analyzed in Gorga (1991a), an unpublished paper which, as a referee of the *Journal of Economic Theory* recognized, contains a "new analytic engine" (*Anon.* 1991). Over time, the growth of values of production, distribution, and consumption leaves behind traces of motion that are an indication of their inner dynamics. Monetary wealth (MW) can be expected to soon leave the initial condition of equilibrium (0, 0, 0) and, spurred by the relative facility with which monetary instruments can be produced, grows at a faster rate than the trajectory of real wealth (RW). Also, since the pattern of distribution of ownership rights over real and monetary wealth is known to remain rather static over time; their trajectories can be represented by a straight line identified as DO. Over time, eliminating all (short and long term, cyclical, random, or aperiodic) loops, breaks, and turns, the system as a whole can be expected to leave behind idealized trajectories as in this figure:

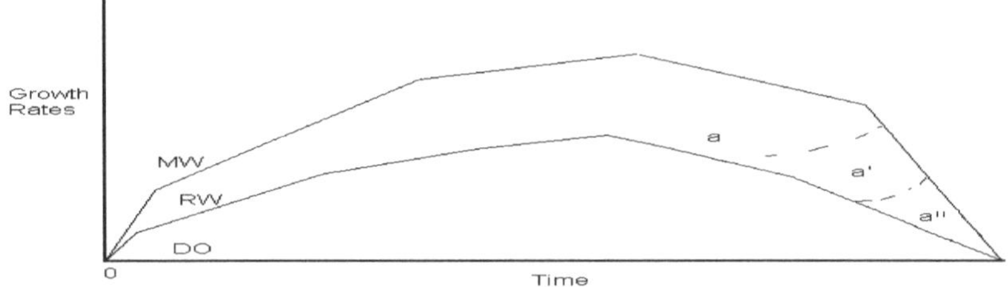

Figure 6. Trajectories of the System as a Whole.

The separation of monetary from real values becomes evident in this figure, which finally gives the definition of the "bubble". Substituting equations and real numbers for the lines of each figure reproduced above, this framework of analysis will acquire predictive value. For instance, area "a"—with its alternative sub-areas a' and a"— attempts to describe the condition of disequilibrium that gradually develops between monetary and real wealth and suggests that the smaller this area, the smaller the loss of real income over time. How to close the gap between the real and the monetary economy in the shortest possible time is clearly a problem of control, namely, a problem of economic policy—the problem of creating a just and sustainable economy.

Updating Economic Policy

Ever since economics was intellectually separated from morality, economic policy has become so rudderless as to lose any sense of direction. The formulation of economic policy has been abandoned to the various schools of economic thought, which, in the presence of the ongoing crisis in economic theory, are unavoidably guided, in ascending order, by petty party politics, ideology, and philosophy. And the practice of economic policy has been abandoned to bankers (as far as monetary policy is concerned) and politicians (as far as fiscal policy is concerned). Definitely there is no integrated policy concerning the stewardship of our natural resources; no integrated industrial policy; no integrated labor policy. The discovery of the economics of Moses and Jesus leaves not one scintilla of doubt: For economic policy to recover its sense of direction, it has to fill the chasm between what is and what ought to be.

The transmission belt that for millennia has carried economic theory into economic policy is the theory of economic justice. This is a theory that, while remaining astonishingly constant as a framework of analysis from Aristotle to the Doctors of the Church, allowed for continuous adaptations to the circumstances of the moment. It was divided into two planks: distributive and commutative justice. Distributive justice guided rules and regulations that govern the division of wealth once it is created; commutative justice guided rules and regulations that govern the transferal of wealth between buyers and sellers at the moment of the exchange. While the Doctors of the Church left much room for discretion in the determination of distributive justice to the parties involved in the economic process, they reached a very specific conclusion as to the dictates of commutative justice: The commutation of wealth, namely the exchange of wealth occurs in accordance with principles of justice only if it occurs on the basis of a free market price—a price determined in a market not dominated by monopolistic forces.

This robust theory was silently decapitated with the separation of economics from morality fully operated by Adam Smith—and, in part, by some of his precursors and nearly all his followers (see Fanfani, 2003, esp. p. 121). The theory of economic justice has disappeared from our consciousness; what we hear is only a faint echo of its splendor in the vague aspirations of the doctrines of "social justice". Truth to tell, the act of decapitation was facilitated by the fact that the theory of economic justice was never presented with a visible head. People with direct or, through the commons (for millennia the safety valve to preserve the dignity of the poor), indirect access to land and natural resources participated in the economic process as a matter of fact and as a consequence of an unspoken set of rights. Hence, it never occurred to Aristotle or the Doctors of the Church to make explicit the requirements of a third plank that might be called participative justice (Gorga 1999). For a great variety of reasons, those conditions are no longer in existence. Today, one has to beg in order to participate in the economic process. And if one does not take part in it, one is marginalized; one is shunted to the margins of society. Hence the plank of participative justice must be added explicitly to the theory of economic justice. Once that is done, one is presented with a framework of analysis that can be represented as follows:

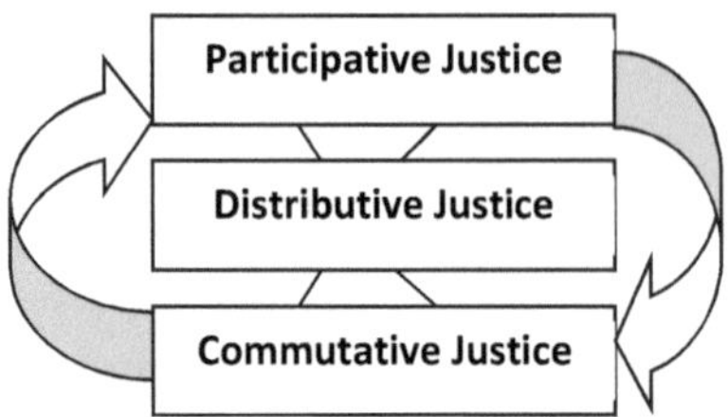

Figure 7. Economic Justice

As it can be seen, figure 7 is a mirror image of figure 6. Since the distribution of ownership rights is an inherent part of the economic process, economic justice is a natural extension of economics. One can just as soon separate the economic process from the theory of economic justice as one can separate a person from his shadow. Given this condition, a minimum set of questions to be asked in the evaluation of any economic policy are the following ones: Does the proposed policy favor participation in the creation of wealth? Does it allow for a fair distribution of the wealth thus created? Does it allow for a fair transfer of wealth from one person to another? This is the way we are going to insert the principles informing the economics of Moses and the economics of Jesus into the economic structure of the modern world.

Staying away from broad and elaborate discussions does not necessarily imply the wisdom of staying away from the specifics of the case. The specific question is: How can we transfer the principles of economic justice into the complexities of the modern economy?

Updating Economic Practice

The transmission belt that carries the theory of economic justice into practice, and shapes objective guidelines for the formulation and evaluation of just economic policies, is the reality of economic rights and economic responsibilities. They come forward as responses to the well-known requirements of the factors of production identified by Classical economists as land, capital, and labor—with the addition of a distinction between financial capital and physical capital. Our focus of attention is on the plank of participative justice; successive iterations that are mostly skipped in this presentation would reveal that the same economic rights and responsibilities satisfy also the requirements of the planks of distributive and commutative justice. A minimal set of economic rights and corresponding responsibilities is as follows.

1. *We all have the right of access to land and natural resources.* This is a natural right. It belongs to us just in virtue of our humanness. Land and natural resources are our original commons. They belong to all. This is an essential right, because without the possibility of exercising it, we are deprived of the possibility of participating in the economic process. And without this participation, we are marginalized; we are made dependent on the good will of others. The most direct way of securing this right in the complexity of the modern world is through the exercise of **the responsibility to pay taxes** for the exclusive use of those resources that are under our command (cf. Kelly 2004))—with a corresponding reduction of taxes on buildings and man-made improvements on the land. Land that sits idle does not produce income, yet it produces capital appreciation over time. Land taxation is the economic bridge between hoarding, namely the accumulation of idle land, and the right of access to that land with its natural resources. Paying taxes on the value of land and natural resources gradually encourages dis-hoarding, hence it lowers the price of the land, and correspondingly opens up the resources of that land to all those who need them and can make use of them. Worrisome hoarding is especially that which occurs both downtown and in the belt surrounding major cities and towns: it is to leapfrog over this belt that people go to the suburbs in search for affordable land, thus creating overstretched lines of communication and protection and overlong commuting lines—with consequent waste of fuel that overtaxes nonrenewable resources, the ozone layer, and the pocketbook. Paying taxes on land values is a most fair form of taxation, because it implies returning to the community part of the value that is created, not by the individual owner, but by the community. And still there is no compulsion in this policy: pay more taxes and keep control over more land. In fact, it can even be said that this mechanism is an equivalent of the original Jubilee concerning land. (To see how this pair meets also the requirements of distributive and commutative justice, let us simply consider that, if one avoids taxes, the total tax load is not going to be distributed fairly among the population. And if one avoids taxes, one obtains something—i.e., private control over a quantity of resources—for which he does not offer proportionate compensation to the rest of the community.)

When fully explored in its dynamic elements, it will be seen that the eventual implementation of this first set of economic rights and responsibilities leads to the creation of a just and sustainable national economic policy concerning the utilization of land and natural resources.

2. *We all have the right of access to national credit.* Since national credit is the power of a nation to create money, and since the value of money is given by the value of wealth left over by past generations and the creativity of every person in a nation, national credit is the last frontier, the last commons. Without access to credit today one is made economically impotent. Worse, since this advantage is automatically granted to the privileged few, it is automatically denied to the majority of the population who are henceforth condemned to pay a higher rate of interest, if they obtain credit at all. Of course, such a loan should be extended only on the basis of **the responsibility to repay the loan**. And these loans will have a high chance of being repaid because they ought to be issued at cost and issued exclusively to individually owned and operated enterprises, Employee Stock Ownership Plans (ESOPs), and cooperatives (and states and municipalities) and issued exclusively for capital formation, namely for the creation of new wealth—not to buy financial paper, consumer goods or goods to be hoarded. Capital credit liberates people, while consumer credit enslaves them.

When fully explored in its dynamic elements, it will be seen that the eventual implementation of this second set of economic rights and responsibilities leads to the creation of a just and sustainable national economic policy concerning the utilization of our financial resources.

3. *We all have the right to the fruits of our labor.* This right should not be limited to the right to obtain only a wage. It should be extended to cover the other major fruit of economic growth over time: capital appreciation—as well as being subject to capital loss, of course. The only justification for reserving the right to capital appreciation to stockholders, the owners of a corporation, and excluding workers from it, can be found in the fact that loans are given only to owners of past wealth (the Catch-22 of today's economic reasoning: "save and invest and you too can become rich"—as if this were either economically feasible or an ecologically sustainable proposition). But from now on this right can be extended to people who do not have prior wealth through the right of access to national credit—especially by legally transforming workers into owners through individually owned enterprises, Employee Stock Ownership Plans (ESOPs), and cooperatives. Of course, this full right should be extended only in correspondence with **the responsibility to offer services** of value equivalent to projected compensation. And

there will be an outpouring of such services because, while in a command and control economy workers are requested to check their brain at the factory gate, in a moral economy workers/owners are legally and psychologically empowered to exercise their brain fully at their work post. Indeed, by linking costs of production with individual producers, current incentives to overextend business enterprises and to overexploit land, natural, and financial resources will be abated.

When fully explored in its dynamic elements, it will be seen that the eventual implementation of this third set of economic rights and responsibilities leads to the creation of a just and sustainable national economic policy concerning the utilization of our labor resources.

4. *We all have the right to protect our wealth.* This right seems to be universally accepted, except in one case that matters most: in the case of the trustification process, the process used especially after the Civil War in the United States to create corporate trusts and repeated in a hundred subtle variations ever since all over the world. (People felt free, not only to acquire shares of the stock of one corporation, but free to use that stock to acquire another whole corporation by all forms of trusts, mergers, and acquisition. The very idea of the corporation, forever a public entity, was then privatized and monetized.) There are two ways in which most corporations grow: One is through internal growth, and this approach ought to be protected in no uncertain terms; the other is growth by external purchase, and this manifestation ought to be prohibited in no uncertain terms. Why? Because this prohibition is the only certain way to protect the wealth of present owners. And if it is assumed that most stockholders of the modern corporation are happy to have their shares bought and sold on the market, it must be granted that growth-by-purchase takes wealth away from workers who have contributed to create that value—and many times, in the trustification process, lose their work site as well. All in the name of efficiency— a misnomer that stands for private financial gain generated at the expense of shifting costs onto the community. Of course, this right ought to be purchased only at the cost of **the responsibility to respect the wealth of others**. These are two way streets. We cannot even attempt to restrain the Pac-Man economy, while we use Pac-Man instruments.

When fully explored in its dynamic elements, it will be seen that the eventual implementation of this fourth set of economic rights and responsibilities leads to the creation of a just and sustainable national economic policy concerning the utilization of our physical capital resources.

Somewhat more detailed analyses of these economic rights and responsibilities are contained in Gorga (1959, 1964, 1987, 1988, 1991b, 1994, 1997, 1999, and 2002). These economic rights and responsibilities can be applied by everyone who does not only want to receive economic justice, but also wants to grant economic justice to everyone else. Operating as tipping points (Gladwell 2000) in our reasoning and *modus vivendi*, they will allow us to extend economic freedom to all. A process of mutual interdependence will be set in place to respect not only the reality of economic affairs, but especially the reality of human relationships. Income and wealth will be distributed fairly. There will not be any need for redistribution programs; as an added bonus, lacking fuel at both ends, violent oscillations in the business cycle will be abated.

We will then recover the essential truth of the economics of Moses and the economics of Jesus. This is the truth that that there are two essential conditions of growth: economic freedom and economic justice (as concrete expressions of freedom and morality). The relationship between them is quite clear: While freedom does not necessarily bring justice with it, justice unavoidably brings freedom. One can abuse freedom, one can never abuse justice. Hence, the initial condition of freedom is proof positive of the existence of economic justice in the land.

Conclusion

The economics of Jesus is a restatement of the economics of Moses that can be applied right now, because, in the end, economics is not a dismal science, or the science of making the rich richer. It is a moral science. And, as a science, it can be applied everywhere; it can be applied by everyone—allowing us to tend our vineyard in sheer jubilation for being alive.

By casting away the economics of avarice, envy, and grumbling, if we consistently apply just economic policies for at least ten years we will discover that abject poverty disappears from the face of the earth and the rich grow steadily richer, all the while the despoliation of the land is abated. The reason for this prediction is clear. With economic freedom at large in the land, people will start producing all the wealth that they need. (Indeed, they will start creating only the children they can possibly love.) And since they will directly bear the costs associated with such production, they will produce just what they need—and not one whiff more. The avoidance of inefficiency and waste will be the lodestar to guide production as well as consumption of wealth. Mother earth with her flowers and trees and beasts will be rediscovered as the gentle giver of life and will again be considered as sacred—sacred, just as men and women are sacred; just as the whole universe is sacred.

One disclaimer concerning originality is due at this point. Having labored in the vineyard delimited by the proposition that investment is income minus hoarding for about forty years and discovering, not just while writing this paper, but only while writing the appropriate paragraph in this paper that, rather than being an original proposition, that was the fundamental proposition of the Parable of the Talents, this writer is perhaps beginning to learn how to listen (Ps 95:7-11), and these final considerations are a first result of this listening. Just as the economics of Moses and the economics of Jesus belong to Moses and to Jesus, so their translation into economic theory belongs to Keynes on the one hand and the probing questioning of Franco Modigliani on the other; and their translation into economic policy belongs to Benjamin Franklin, Henry George, Louis D. Brandeis, and Louis O. Kelso. To be noticed is that this economic policy is an all-American affair.

Appendix A

On the Modern Attempt at Separating Economics from Morality

From Moses to Adam Smith everyone agreed that economic activity occurs within the context of the moral law—thus continuing without a hiatus the tradition of the Jewish Law. Enter Adam Smith, a professor, not of economics, but of moral philosophy and—at first following and then leading, a whole set of well-known complex historical and cultural events—economics becomes separated from morality. No matter what he said in his *Theory of Moral Sentiments*, a work that very few have ever read, in the *Wealth of Nations*, the foundation stone of modern economics, Adam Smith makes no reference to economic justice and five references to morality, all offensively disparaging. No wonder he was unable to fulfill his promise to write a treatise that would potentially unify all social sciences (1759, last par.; 1790, A2). Gradually the importance of morality in economics does not only go unrecognized; it is firmly denied. This breach in such a long tradition has been bored into our minds through this doubt: Does not morality lead to inefficiency? So deep is this bore that, in the name of economic efficiency, namely a presumed inefficiency of morality (please notice the unspoken subtle change of words), the Immoral Economy is tolerated at nearly every level of the discussion. Just as Jesus cast away the money changers from the Temple of his day, so he would certainly cast away the word changers from the temple of thought of today. The Immoral Economy is not tenable—neither from an economic point of view nor from an intellectual point of view.

The Immoral Economy Is not Tenable from an Economic Point of View

The assumption of a presumed inefficiency of morality is so central to modern thinking yet so contrary to the composition of reality that one marvels how it can receive such widespread submissive assent. The assumption is based, not on sound macroeconomic reasoning and comprehensive accounting, but on a series of blatant shortcuts. At the very core of economic theory there is a transposition of the tool of measurement with the object of measurement. The tool of measurement is money; the object of measurement is economic activity. Because of the transposition of these two elements, everything in mainstream economics is reduced to money—and human beings, if they enter the equations at all, are reduced to rational automatons. The most immediate effect of this shortcut is that the monetary economy obliterates the vision of the real economy: in mainstream economics there is no accounting of stocks of natural resources or stocks of real goods and services. No wonder Wall Street analysts reduce the whole of economics to the "bottom line" and everyone is expected to give assent to their valuation. Please note that the vaunted economic efficiency is thus reduced to monetary efficiency. The consequences of this reduction, just as the consequences of the reduction of biology to sex, are shunted aside by a shortsighted understanding and a deficient measurement of efficiency: first, the efficiency of the Gross National Product is always measured in the short run, whereby the cost of depressions and recessions is not taken into account; second, the measurement of the efficiency of the Gross National Product does not take into account the Gross National Cost represented by overexploitation of the land and of human beings, who are treated like commodities/machines requested to work harder and harder, faster and faster—or are cast aside onto the sidewalks of our cities and towns; third, the efficiency of the firm does not take into account the cost of externalities, an economic category that insulates the firm from the rest of society: the more such costs (costs of pollution, costs of pension plans, medical costs) are calculated as external to the firm, the better it is for the bottom line of course; and, finally, the cost of labor does not take into account the cost of welfare programs, most of which issue an essential subsidy to underpaid workers. No wonder monetary efficiency is exalted and economic morality is berated: private interests enjoy all the profits; the general public bears all the costs. Fools are treated like fools. In the reality of economics—the morality of economics—costs can be shifted onto other shoulders, but they do not go away. The unity of economics and morality is a matter internal to the economic system; it can be hidden but it cannot be destroyed. The Immoral Economy is not an economic necessity determined by "efficiency"—quite the contrary. Clearly, the Immoral Economy is not the result of "blind forces"; it is not the result of an "invisible hand". The Immoral Economy is the result of immoral choices by the hands of very visible human beings.

The Immoral Economy Is Not Tenable from an Intellectual Point of View

The battering ram used to transform the small, no matter how unfounded, doubt about the inefficiency of morality into the rout of morality has been a peculiar understanding of freedom. Insulated from the rest of the universe, this word has been insulated from rational analysis. Would I release to you control over my freedom? Certainly not! The beginning of wisdom lies in the realization that neither words nor even sentences stand alone. Do two parallel lines meet?

The modern understanding of freedom, in fact, is propped up with a web of intellectual relationships that has gradually yielded the construction of a full-fledged system of thought known as modern rationalism. When individual propositions are analyzed as part of this system of thought, they do not stand to reason. In this system of thought, morality is reduced to a null set because the meaning of freedom has become so tenuous, so empty of content as to be elevated to the rank of infinity; the idea of freedom has been raised to such altitudes as to become an absolute value. This elevation is made plausible because the entire intellectual system of rationalism, just like modern economic analysis that stands at its core, is ahistorical. If observed in the reality of history, it becomes incontrovertible that freedom in general and economic freedom in particular is not absolute. First of all, unbridled economic freedom is a good that is restricted for the consumption of the few; indeed, unbridled economic freedom for the few is acquired at the cost of subjection for the many. If it were an absolute value, unbridled freedom would be able to be extended to all. Those who disagree with this statement are compelled to admit to the existence of different degrees of freedom. Yet, again, if it were an absolute value, unbridled freedom would be able to be extended to all in identical parts. By the same token, if it were an absolute value, unbridled freedom's life would be extended forever.

The historic evidence to the contrary is provided by economic dynamics—more than any other discipline. The evidence is so rich one marvels how the elevation of freedom to such height can receive so little examination and so widespread submissive assent. Freedom is not enough for sustainable growth. On the contrary, the repeated history of business enterprise upon business enterprise and indeed the apparent history of entire civilizations show that unbridled freedom inevitably leads to libertinism, which gradually destroys freedom and then civilization itself.

The destruction of enterprises and the destruction of civilizations might take some time. There are other effects that are immediate. The elevation of freedom to the status of an absolute carries with it the destruction, not so much of religion—which is wanted and expected—as the destruction of the sense of community. Isolated rational automatons (more commonly called economic agents, individuals, and disembodied minds), which stand at the basis of modern rationalism and especially at the basis of modern economic theory, clearly have no sense of community. It is only this lack of sense of community that ultimately explains the use of such blatant shortcuts to measure efficiency as the ones mentioned above. Automatons have no sense of responsibility toward the community. Indeed, they have no feelings; no sentiments. And as such they ultimately destroy the dignity of the human race at its deepest core.

Economics Cannot Be Separated from Morality

True efficiency is the result of morality. Economics cannot be separated from morality. Let us immediately rephrase that. Economics cannot be separated from morality without creating negative economic consequences that generally vary in accordance with the seriousness of the moral transgression. As human beings we are free, because we are called to choose—not between Gucci and Pucci—but between good and evil.

Morality is the set of rules that train the will to desire and to achieve what is positive for oneself and for others, by reconciling within oneself the forces of both freedom and authority. An undisciplined will suggests that if I steal I clearly add to my wealth. That would appear to be a positive result for me, even though negative for you. Ancient moral rules suggest that to steal is an immoral act, hence to be shunned, because it is not good for one's dignity.

Human dignity is not an abstraction. Not to have dignity means not to be fully human. Not to be fully human means to be either like beasts, thereby having no creativity and no freedom, or like stones thereby having no feelings of pain or joy in addition to no freedom.

Appendix B

Hoarding for Doubters

This writer has spent many years in the vineyard delimited by the proposition that Investment is Income minus Hoarding. And still he tends to lose sight of the fact that, for many complex reasons, most economists do not—and cannot—see hoarding. They do not physically see hoarding; hence, they intellectually deny its existence. The issue is not one of economics. The issue is one of mathematics and logic: once the economic reality is described by the given definitions of saving and consumption, saving becomes "equal" to investment (cf. Keynes 1936, p. 63), and no space is left for hoarding. It is to be noted that, as demonstrated in the text, hoarding was well known and widely discussed from Jesus to Locke.

Due to the new framework of analysis designed by this writer (Gorga 2002, pp. 23-40, 67-158, 303-328), it is again possible to speak of hoarding within the context of formal economic theory. Many consequences ensue from the existence of hoarding (cf. *ibid.,* pp. 235-302, 329-358). Yet, even accepting the validity of the new intellectual construction that includes hoarding in its purview, a doubt persists about the existence of hoarding (see Broski 2003).

This doubt is creating an interesting consequence that can be explained only in terms of the relationship between intellectual paradigms and real phenomena. Thomas E. Kuhn in *The Structure of Scientific Revolutions* pointed out that the prevailing paradigm in physics for a long time made scientists see a substance, phlogiston, which eventually turned out to be a non-existent element. In economics today, there is a reverse chain of causation. Since economists deny the existence of hoarding, they tend to conclude that there is no reason for a new intellectual construction such as elaborated in Gorga (2002) that unarguably, again, permits its vision.

This Appendix therefore attempts to clarify three questions: What is hoarding? Is there any hoarding? Who does the hoarding? This exposition also makes it clear that hoarding has a direct effect on both the projection of future economic activity and the understanding of the General Theory.

What Is Hoarding?

Hoarding is the act of keeping wealth in an idle state. Hoarding is the act of keeping wealth in an idle state *for any reason apart from a technical requirement for keeping it idle*. More specifically, hoarded is all wealth that is not used, *at the moment of the observation*, as a consumer good or a capital good. Before starting the discussion, we shall equip ourselves with an ad hoc methodology and a minimalist economic theory that will allow us to find hoarding.

Ad Hoc Methodology on How to Find Hoarding

We shall abstract from the theoretical possibility or impossibility of the existence of hoarding. We shall be totally indifferent to either one of these two theoretical possibilities.

In other words, the primary focus of this Appendix is not on any of the causes or the effects of hoarding, nor on its relationships with the canonical constellation of the component elements of economic theory, but on hoarding in itself and by itself. Yet, nothing stands alone. Therefore, at times we shall call attention to some effects of hoarding; and, given that any economic action has effects on quantities and relative prices, we shall reason by excess. Whenever necessary and appropriate, we shall run a peculiar thought experiment (cf. Kuhn 1996, p. 88); we shall assume that the entire stock of a particular item of wealth falls under the exclusive control of only one person.

A Minimalist Theory

As an inescapable consequence of the given definition of hoarding, all wealth is posited to be divided into three parts: consumer goods, capital goods, and goods hoarded. This is a minimalist theory, but a theory nonetheless. The assumption is that any item of wealth—not simply money—can be hoarded.

What Is Hoarded

Currency. Currency hoarded is the simplest case to identify. Currency under the mattress in excess of the need for daily transactions, as well as currency kept in a safe deposit box, is money hoarded. It is money kept idle. A more complex variant of this phenomenon is money that is owned by a bank while keeping it idle in a safe deposit box. That currency is also hoarded. Let us remember that the object of our observation is the specific item of wealth, not its owner, and that here we are not primarily concerned with either the causes or the effects of hoarding.

Land. Land hoarded is simple to identify. All land that is used neither as a consumer good (e.g., for recreational purposes) nor as a capital good is land hoarded. Land that is kept idle for the esthetic pleasure of looking at it is not land hoarded but land used as any other consumer good. All land that a government keeps idle for recreational purposes is not land hoarded; yet land in an unvisited park is land hoarded. Land covered with weeds and rubbish in the downtown of a city is clearly land hoarded. All uncultivated and undeveloped (landlocked) land is also hoarded. All land kept idle in a country in which there are idle hands that would till or somehow make use of it, is land that is clearly hoarded; see, e.g. latifundia.

Gold. Gold in the course of extraction and sale in a gold mine is a capital good. Gold in a microchip plant or a jeweler's workshop is also a capital good. An interesting case is the case of a gold bracelet in a jeweler's shop: this is still a capital good. It is only when the bracelet adorns a woman's wrist that the item becomes a consumer good. And what is a gold ingot at Fort Knox if not, clearly, a good hoarded? And so is the gold ingot in the safe of a bank, whether a private person or the bank itself happens to be its owner.

Supplies. Supplies are clearly capital goods; yet, even supplies can be hoarded—as they are when they are bought and kept idle for a period of time that goes beyond technical reasons for keeping them idle. One might say that when the physical flow of supplies is changed into a stock of supplies, chances are that those supplies are hoarded. When in the 70s oil was kept in tankers waiting outside harbors, that oil was hoarded. Some of this oil was hoarded to staunch the effect of expected higher prices; some of it was hoarded in fear of future exhaustion of those supplies. The reason does not matter. It is the economic condition that matters.

A coffee cup. A coffee cup in my home is a consumer good. A coffee cup in my office is a capital good. And a coffee cup in my attic is a good hoarded—unless I use it, even just once a year, on my patio during summertime.

Consumer goods. The hardest case to identify as hoarding, at least the last case that was identified by this writer, is the case of the hoarding of consumer goods. (Unless the eyes are never peeled away from the economic reality, words become utterly misleading.) Again the case of voluntary hoarding is clear. The case of the person who buys two pairs of boots because prices are skyrocketing is clear: one pair is used as consumer goods and the other is hoarded. More subtle is the case of unanticipated hoarding. Have you ever discovered in your clothes closet a shirt with its price tag still attached after a couple of years of its purchase? The item was clearly hoarded. More deviant still is the case of "consumer goods" that have lost their utility to the owner, and are hoarded because one is too lazy to offer them to others who would put them to good use.

Any item of wealth can be hoarded. During the Great Inflation of the 70s Johnny Carson, the famous comedian, one night made a joke about the disappearance of tissue paper. The day after the shelves were bare. A shortage was created because of the unexpected demand. Indeed, much of the gasoline shortage those same years was created by the fact that many drivers would tend to keep the tank constantly filled. They were hoarding gasoline.

Stocks and bonds. Stocks and bonds are not wealth; they represent wealth. Therefore, they cannot be hoarded—even though the corporation in whose name those stocks and bonds are issued might be hoarding some real wealth on its own account. No matter how many consequences derive from accumulating even all the stock of a corporation, this action does not directly affect other people's wealth; at the limit, you can destroy all the stock certificates that you own, and you do not directly affect other people's wealth. Other people would benefit from a transfer of the title of ownership of these certificates to them, but that is a moral issue with its own indirect economic consequences. Directly, the wealth of the nation would not even minimally be affected by the destruction or transfer of stocks and bonds; indirectly, you might increase the value of the remaining stock certificates, but that would only be a monetary change. Currency is significantly different from stocks and bonds. To say the least, currency has an immediate and direct utility. Accumulate or destroy all currency, and you do not destroy the value of any real wealth; yet you immediately make all exchanges more cumbersome and gradually more expensive. As a saying once went, currency saves shoe leather. This is the cost—in real wealth—that would be incurred by the nation if all currency were destroyed.

Labor. To evaluate the full cost of hoarding incurred by a nation, one has to realize that involuntary unemployment is labor power that is hoarded. To reach an accurate measurement of this phenomenon, one has to keep in mind, first, that official unemployment rates from the ghettos to the Indian Reservations generally vary anywhere from 15% to 75%; second, that official statistics measure unemployment only among those who are still actively searching for employment: those who have given up are not counted. Another group that might be worth to look at with new eyes is the pool of officially retired people.

Is There Hoarding?

The specific question is: Is there any hoarding any time, anywhere in the world? To answer this question in relation to money, it is important to bring to mind two specific examples. First, the less developed the banking system in a country, the more hoarding takes place under the mattress. The deeper the condition of economic depression in a country, the higher the accumulation of money hoarded in a bank— by a bank. How much deeper did the Great Depression become because banks could not find borrowers for their hoards?

To clearly see hoarding, one has to make a dynamic and longitudinal analysis of the issue. One will then discover that the quantity of certain forms of hoarding increases over time. During the same period, other forms decrease: currency, for instance, is hoarded less when the prices of goods rise. (This is another variation of Gresham's Law.) But of course the calculation has to take into account that the amount of currency in circulation depends on the will of the people as well as the willingness of the monetary system to accommodate that demand. The condition is wholly dynamic. And since in economics everything is instantaneously related to everything else, one is always faced with questions of relative values and relative prices.

These observations lead to another consideration. At first sight, one might be tempted to assume that all hoarding is "bad" or more specifically that all hoarding has negative economic effects. That is not necessarily the case. Some hoarding might cause positive effects for the individual person as well as for society as a whole. For instance, some undeveloped and uncultivated (landlocked) land might become a buried treasure for the next generation; and some money kept in a safe deposit box keeps prices rising even minimally at a slower pace. There are no general cases in economics; all cases are individual ones. That is why one cannot let "the market" make decisions for oneself.

Who Does the Hoarding?

We all hoard wealth. Some more, some less, but we all hoard wealth. Even in this brief excursus we have met governments hoarding gold, landlords hoarding land, bankers hoarding currency, industrialists hoarding supplies, and individual human beings hording consumer goods. A disclosure: This writer hoards books and computers: there are some books that he knows full well he will never get to read or no longer needs to read; there are some computers that he knows full well he will never get to use—he should give them away, instead he hoards them.

Some Concluding Comments

The existence of hoarding is proof positive of the existence of freedom, rather than determinism, in the world of economics.

As against the accumulation of goods hoarded, the consumption of consumer goods is, indeed, determined by need: needs of physical survival and needs of social status. The consumption of capital goods is also determined by the need to reduce the amount of time—or, more precisely, the amount of life—one devotes to the production of goods; the resulting free time is proof positive of the efficiency of the economic system in which one lives; to whom and to what one devotes the resulting free time is determined by the degree of civilization and spirituality stored in this person's character.

Is not the existence of hoarding, then, proof positive of the amount of freedom granted to the individual person by the economic system in which one lives? And the amount of dishoarding, by giving one's surplus wealth to the people who need it and cannot produce it for themselves, is proof positive of the degree of morality lived by the person who dishoards.

Clearly, neither consumption nor investment, but hoarding alone is wholly determined by the free will of the individual economic agent.

Hoarding is an arbitrary and subjective activity. Of course, there is much arbitrariness and subjectivity in consumption and investment as well. To say the least, then, hoarding contains a greater degree of arbitrariness and subjectivity than either consumption or investment. At the limit, as we know, differences in degree are differences in kind. Hoarding therefore is an economic activity fundamentally different from consumption and investment.

The discovery of the existence of hoarding in the economic system is not an exclusively intellectual issue. The existence of hoarding has a clear concrete effect on the measurement of economic activity. Hoarding can be measured only by working with an intimate understanding of the person who does the hoarding. All other measurements are purely arbitrary. Any projection of future economic activity that does not take the erratic nature of hoarding into full account is destined to yield only ambiguous results. More generally, any national projection of future economic activity that does not take the existence of hoarding into account is doomed to make false predictions.

It is equally worthwhile to note that the existence of hoarding has a decisive influence on the understanding of the *General Theory*. Hoarding is what fills the gap between the form and the substance of that great masterpiece. While the form is written on the basis of Keynes' model of the economic system as pointed out above, the substance of the General Theory is written in terms of the existence of hoarding. Three major pieces of evidence should suffice. First, if there were no hoarding in the economic system it would make no difference whether people had a propensity to consume a little less than one's income (Keynes 1936, p. 96), because the difference would be taken up by saving and investing. Yet, Keynes knew full well that there is hoarding in the community and therefore he specified that under given circumstances "saving and spending will *both* decrease" (*ibid*. p. 111; italics in original). With the recognition of hoarding, this observation turns out to be true in a static examination of the economic system, as well as in a dynamic investigation of the system. The second case regards Keynes' prescription for the "only radical cure for the crises of confidence which afflict the economic life of the modern world" (*ibid*. p. 161); as analyzed in Gorga (2002, esp. pp. 93-115), the prescription becomes clear only if one takes the existence of hoarding into account. Third,

Keynes defined interest in an outright fashion as "the reward of not-hoarding" (*ibid.* p. 174).

Appendix C

Mathematical Models
A Progressive View of the Economic System

Eliminating all explanations concerning their derivation and the interconnections among them, this Appendix is an attempt to concentrate the mind on the basic mathematical models of the Concordian economics. These models—with key diagrams given in the text—offer a progressive view of the economic system as a whole. This process of discovery is best described by a Fields Medalist at Princeton University, William Thurston (2006, p. D1): "You don't see what you're seeing until you see it, but when you do see it, it lets you see many other things."

Flows Model
(The Revised Keynes' Model)

$$Y = C + S$$
$$I = Y - S$$
$$I = C$$

where
Y stands for Income
C for Consumption or *any* type of expenditure
S for Saving, an entity conceptually separated from Investment
I for Investment

Flows Model
with
Hoarding (H) substituted for Saving

$$Y = C + H$$
$$I = Y - H$$
$$I = C$$

Flows Model
with
Production (P) substituted for Investment

$$Y = C + H$$
$$P = Y - H$$
$$P = C$$

Flows Model
With the Equality of Production and Consumption
Substituted with the Equivalence of Production, Distribution (D), and Consumption

$$Y = C + H$$
$$P = Y - H$$
$$P = D = C$$

Monetary Formulation of the Flows Model

$MY = E + E_h$

$E_k = MY - E_h$

$E_k = E$

where

MY stands for money income

E for expenditure

E_h for hoarding-expenditure, namely, money directly hoarded

and/or spent on goods hoarded

E_k for investment-expenditure

Stocks Model

$$\text{Wealth} = (\text{Consumer Goods} + \text{Capital Goods}) + \text{Goods Hoarded}$$
$$\text{Investment-assets} = \text{Wealth} - \text{Goods Hoarded}$$
$$\text{Investment-assets} = \text{Consumer Goods} + \text{Capital Goods}$$

Model of Production

$$P = CG + KG + GH$$
$$KG = P - (GH + CG)$$
$$KG = OKG$$

where
CG stands for Consumer Goods
KG for Capital Goods
GH for Goods Hoarded
OKG for value of Ownership of Capital Goods

Model of Distribution

$$D = OCG + OKG + OGH$$
$$OKG = D - (OGH + OCG)$$
$$OKG = I$$

where
D stands for Distribution or Real Income observed from the point of view of distribution of ownership rights
OCG for value of Ownership of Consumer Goods
OKG for value of Ownership of Capital Goods
OGH for value of Ownership of Goods Hoarded

Model of Consumption

$$C = E_h + E$$
$$I = C - E_h$$
$$I = E$$

where
C stands for Consumption or Money Income observed
from the point of view of consumption
E_h for money reserved for Hoarding-Expenditure
E for money reserved for Expenditure (on consumer goods and capital goods)
I for Investment

Synthetic Model of the Economic System as a Whole
(From Gorga 1991a)

$$p^{\cdot} = fp(p,d,c)$$
$$d^{\cdot} = fd(p,d,c)$$
$$c^{\cdot} = fc(p,d,c)$$

where

$p^{\cdot}$ stands for rate of change in total production

$d^{\cdot}$ for rate of change in the values of distribution of ownership rights

$c^{\cdot}$ for rate of change in total expenditure.

References

Allen, R. G. D. 1970. *Mathematical Economic,* 2nd ed., London and New York: Macmillan, St. Martin's.

Anon. 1991. "Referee Report, 'The Dynamics of the Economic System,' by Carmine Gorga." *J Econ. Theory*, # 91297.

Brady, Michael Emmett. 2004a. *Essays on J. M. Keynes and...* Xlibris Corporation.

______. 2004b. *J. M. Keynes' Theory of Decision Making, Induction, and Analogy.* Xlibris Corporation.

______. 2006. *The Applied Mathematics of J.M. Keynes' Theory of Effective Demand in the General Theory.* Xlibris Corporation.

Broski, Mark. 2003. "The Economic Process: An Instantaneous Non-Newtonian Picture. Carmine Gorga." *Journal of Markets and Morality* 6, no. 1: 297-98.

Catherine of Siena. 1980. *The Dialogue.* S. Noffke trans. Mahwah NJ: The Paulist Press.

Chapra, Umer M. 1985. *Towards a Just Monetary System.* Leicester, UK: The Islamic Foundation.

Fanfani, Amintore. 2003. Catholicism, Protestantism, and Capitalism. Norfolk, VA: IHS Press.

Foley, Duncan K. 2006. *Adam's Fallacy: A Guide to Economic Theology.* Cambridge, MA/ London, UK: Belknap Press of Harvard University Press.

Gladwell, Malcolm. 2000. *The Tipping Point: How Little Things Can Make a Big Difference.* NY: Little, Brown & Company.

Goldsmith, Raymond W. 1955-1956. *A Study of Saving in the United States*, 3 Vols. Princeton: Princeton University Press.

Gorga, Carmine. 1959. *A Synthesis of the Political Thought of Louis D. Brandeis.* Graduation Dissertation University of Naples.

_____. 1964. "Not Simply a National Fund, but a Stabilization and Development Fund", *Mondo Economico*, 19 (14) 14-16.

_____. 1982. "The Revised Keynes' Model" (an Abstract), Atlantic Econ. J. 10:3, p. 52.

_____and Norman G. Kurland. 1987. "The Productivity Standard: A True Golden Standard," in *Every Worker An Owner: A Revolutionary Free Enterprise Challenge to Marxism,* D. M. Kurland, ed. Washington, DC: Center for Economic and Social Justice.

_____ and Louis J. Ronsivalli. 1988. *Quality Assurance of Seafood.* New York: Van Nostrand Reinhold.

_____. 1991a. "The Dynamics of the Economic System," unpub. man.

_____. 1991b. "Bold New Directions in Politics and Economics," *The Human Economy Newsletter,* 12:1, pp. 3-6, 12.

_____ . 1994. "Four Economic Rights: Social Renewal Through Economic Justice for All," *Social Justice Rev.* 85:1-2, pp. 3-6.

_____ and Stuart B. Weeks. 1997. "Fisheries Renewal: A Renewal of the Soul of Business," *Catholic Social Science Rev.* 2, pp. 145-161.

_____ . 1998. "The Creators of Poverty," *Gloucester Daily Times,* **Symposium**, December 18, p. A10.

_____ . 1999. "Toward the Definition of Economic Rights," *J. Markets and Morality,* 2:1, pp. 88-101.

_____ . 2002. *The Economic Process: An Instantaneous Non-Newtonian Picture.* Lanham, MD and Oxford: University Press of America.

Harris, Maria. 1996. *Proclaim Jubilee! A Spirituality for the Twenty-First Century.* Louisville, KY: Westminster John Knox Press.

Hayek, Friedrick A. 1963. "The Economics of the 1930s as Seen from London," in *Contra Keynes and Cambridge: Essays and Correspondence* (vol. 9 of *The Collected Works of F. A. Hayek*), Bruce Caldwell, ed. 49. Chicago: University of Chicago Press (1995).

______. 1994. *Hayek on Hayek: An Autobiographical Dialogue.* Stephen Kresge and Leif Wenar, eds. Chicago: University of Chicago Press.

Quoted in Bruce Caldwell, *Hayek's Challenge: An Intellectual Biography of F. A. Hayek.* Chicago: University of Chicago Press, 2004, p. 401.

Kelly, John L. 2004. "The Tithe: Land Rent to God," *Acton Institute Religion & Liberty,* July and August.

Keynes, J. Maynard. 1936. *The General Theory of Employment, Interest, and Money.* NY: Harcourt.

______. 1973. *The Collected Writings of John Maynard Keynes,* D. E. Moggridge, ed., Vol. XIV (London, New York and Toronto: Macmillan, St. Martin's Press.
Kuhn, Thomas S. 1996 ed. *The Structure of Scientific Revolutions.* Chicago and London: University of Chicago Press.

Locke, John. 1698. *Two Treatises of Government.* London: Awnsham and John Churchill. Laslett P. ed. NY: A Mentor Book (1965).

Modigliani, Franco. 1980. *The Collected Papers of Franco Modigliani. Vol. 1: Essays in Macroeconomics.* Abel, A. ed. Cambridge MA and London, UK: MIT Press.

Samuelson, Paul A. 1946. "The General Theory," in *Keynes' General Theory: Reports of Three Decades,* R. Lekachman, ed. (New York and London: St. Martin's, Macmillan Press, 1964).

Schumpeter, Joseph A. 1936. "The general theory of employment, interest and money," *J. Amer. Statistical Assoc.* 31, pp. 791-95.
Smith, Adam. 1759. *The Theory of Moral Sentiments.* London: A. Millar, 1790. Sixth edition.

_____. 1776. *An Inquiry into the Nature and Causes of the Wealth of Nations.* London: Methuen and Co., Ltd., ed. Edwin Cannan, 1904. Fifth edition.

Tierney, Brian. 1959. *Medieval Poor Law: A Sketch of Canonical Theory and Its Application in England.* Berkeley: University of California Press.

Thompson, J. M. T. 1986. *Nonlinear Dynamics and Chaos, Geometric Methods for Engineers and Scientists.* New York: Wiley.

Thurston, William. 2006. Quoted in Dennis Overbye, "An Elusive Proof and Its Elusive Prover: That rabbit is actually a sphere. (Read on.) But the man who proved it is missing," *New York Times*, August 15.

Trocmé, André. 1973. *Jesus and the Nonviolent Revolution.* Scottdale PA, Kitchener: Ont.: Herald Press.

Wood, Diane. 2002. *Medieval Economic Thought.* Cambridge, UK: Cambridge University Press.

Zona, Guy A. 1994. *The Soul Would Have No Rainbow if the Eyes had no Tears – and Other Native American Proverbs.* N.Y: Simon and Schuster.

Chapter 6: The Lender Is Not A Hoarder.
And What Is Interest?

I am not a Jew.

How to staunch the river(S) of opprobrium poured over the head of the lender during the last 5,000 years of recorded history?

The Lender Is Not a Hoarder

Even Shakespeare got into the act. Who can forget Shylock? To understand Shakespeare, we have to put him within two bookends: The near universal misquotation of the First Epistle of Paul to Timothy and the forgery of the Protocols of the Elders of Zion. The details are too well known and too painful to recite here.

The first obvious observation to make, and to stress, is that not all the lenders are Jews.

Period.

The second observation to stress is that neither Shakespeare nor those who misquote Paul are economists. They simply do not know what they are talking about. They know not what money is.

A silly point. I am not a Jew. I am not writing this long overdue re-evaluation of the lender because I am a Jew and somehow want desperately to put the record of antisemitism straight at least as the lending of money is concerned.

No. My evaluation of the lender is based on the study of Concordian economics. Through Concordian economics it becomes exceedingly clear that the lender is not a hoarder.

The long bill of particulars against the hoarder is not of concern here.

The long bill of particulars in favor of the lender can be shortened here by asking: Would the world be better off if people with money, people with money who do not have an immediate use for it, were to hoard the money? The question answers itself.

What Can We Demand of the Lender?

No, I am not going to proffer an indiscriminate approval of the actions of the lender. Especially after witnessing the abuses of the lending power of large corporations committed before the last financial crash, when loans were approved for people who could clearly not sustain the load, but nonetheless offered a variety of immediate profits to the lender, it is evident that "society" must demand that the lender use judgmst in the evaluation of the loan.

The lender has responsibilities.

Loans that have minimal chance of being repaid ought not to be issued at all. I wonder whether society will ever find adequate sanctions against irresponsible lending practices, but we can certainly summarily spotlight them and condemn them at will

The second condition through which society must evaluate lending practices is the amount and form of interest to be applied to a loan. To answer these questions appropriately, we need to know what interest is.

What Is Interest?

Interest, Keynes said, is "the reward of not-hoarding." Keynes, of course, is the supreme economist of the last century. The dead economist who controls our lives. All mainstream economics is based on his fundamental book titled the General Theory; all heterodox economics, in its various shapes and forms of "post-Keynesian" economics, as well as Austrian economics, is all economics written "against Keynes."

In the meantime, no one has paid attention to Keynes' definition of interest, because no modern economist understands what hoarding is.

Rather than demanding an effort to understand hoarding, I will be satisfied if the reader makes an effort to understand interest. Benjamin Franklin knew, he understood what interest is, and welcomed it. Did he not famously say something like:

"I'm glad to give the other fellow 5%, if I can earn 6%."

But notice that our Beloved Benjamin, if my love for him gives me permission to be so disrespectful, was talking of capital credit - not the abyss of consumer credit into which we have lately plunged. Consumer credit is only fruitful for the lender. Yet, the loan agreement is entered voluntarily; apart from advocating for education about economic affairs, there is nothing that economics can do to save the borrower and make the consumer loan productive ... unless one approaches the situation indirectly ... unless the "cash-back" movement becomes truly widespread, unless capitalism becomes truly responsive to the needs of consumers - and its own survival - and so responsible as to elect representative consumers to the Board of Directors of modern business corporations through the legal institution of Consumer Stock Ownership Plans (CSOPs).

That is it. With capital credit, interest is the fruit of the use of other peoples' money. With consumer credit, interest is giving to the lender the fruit of one's own future productivity: A totally destructive activity; how many enterprises are undertaken, how many trees are felled to pay interest on consumer credit? The principal in consumer credit is never likely to be paid back.

And yet, does not the consumer derive the benefit of immediate use of real goods and services? Don't we live in the moment? It might be vain to ask: What's the rush?

To summarize, apart from the abyss of consumer credit, with a loan agreement voluntarily entered into by the majority of the population, would society be better off if money remained in the pocket of a person who does not know, or does not want to go through the pain of making money bear fruit?

Let the lender be finally praised.

Two Caveats

This is not an idiosyncratic blessing of interest. There are two important caveats that I should attach to the unjustly vituperated 5,000-years-old practice of lending money at interest. The first caveat is that society should forever be on the alert against exorbitant interest. My brain is too small to define what an exorbitant rate of interest is. But my heart knows it when it sees it. Yes, my heart bleeds a bit at that sight.

Where blood gushes out of my heart is at the mention of compound interest. I cannot find any justification for compound interest, except in the power of the lender and the power of mathematics. To elaborate on the power of the lender, especially the political power of the lender is fruitless. It will forever be exercised, whether openly or through the subterfuge of clever lawyers and accountants - and legislators, should I whisper?

What must be open to discussion is the justification for compound interest. I find none. Let us run a small thought experiment, an experiment whose conclusions can be easily tested through the inordinate intellectual and financial power of the modern University. Let us pose this alternative to a "perfect" representative sample of lenders: What is fairer, Simple Interest - with its linear growth pattern - or Compound Interest, with its exponential growth pattern?

My suspicion is that most people, to repeat, most lenders, will agree that the linear growth rate is fairer than the exponential growth rate.

Will this exercise become the seed to set loan agreements on a just and sustainable basis? Let us shortly find time to give some undivided attention to the issue. Let us not sheepishly accept diktats from the past.

If this solution is not chosen, especially because its implementation is surely going to be a slow process, rather than advocating a vainglorious attempt to curb the power of individual lenders, let us see what can be done, systematically - as a society.

A Fruitful Curb of the Power of the Lender

Yes, the modern world - ah, Progress, Enlightenment, Reason, and all that - is bereft of defenses against the power of the lender. We have no intellectually solid, no morally valid defense against the power of the lender.

It is scouring the past that I have unearthed "the" solution: The Jubilee Solution. The Jubilee Solution is a systematic cancellation of all debts on the eve of the Jubilee Year. The Jubilee Year starts at the end of the seventh year.

There are various forms of jubilee. There is the Seven Day Jubilee regarding Time; the Seven Year Jubilee regarding the tillage of the Land; and the end of the 7x7 = 49 Year Jubilee regarding Stewardship of the Land. These are all extremely important manifestations of Jubilee, jubilation of the heart. This encompassing vision is too much for one lazy morning. Let us concentrate our attention on the Seven Year Jubilee regarding debt.

Much to say. Compressed, it is this: It is only money, people; it is only money that, remaining in the pocket of the lender, would most likely be hoarded; it is only money that is keeping the debtor in knots; it is only a set of zeroes that, once cancelled from the accounting books, make everyone free to start a new life as a productive agent again. (Have not modern venture capitalists learned not to shy away from first, and second, and even third failure? If the borrower has used the painful experience to learn how to succeed, why waste all that learning?)

It was Moses who legislated the Debt Jubilee. It was Jewish society that had the intellectual talent to see the wisdom of the Debt Jubilee and the moral stamina to practice it every seven years. Cynics doubt the debt Jubilee was ever practiced. I personally do not care whether it was practiced even once and Michael Hudson has provided an unobjectionable wealth of evidence of the soundness of this solution in the number and quality of copycats: Every Emperor, every King - well, most Emperors, most Kings; many Emperors, many Kings ? - upon installation has declared a Debt Jubilee.

Moses was a Jew. And Jesus did not ever contradict Moses, but he asserted his readiness to fulfill the mission of Moses and the Prophets. In the words of Paul, Jesus did not say that money is the root of all evil. The correct quotation is

"Love of money is the root of all evil."

Love of money is the root of hoarding and, in the Parable of the Talents, Jesus, uncharacteristically, sends the hoarder straight to Hell: No trial; no appeal.

Yes, I am not a Jew, but I am very proud to acknowledge my intellectual debt to Moses, and to Jesus.

.

Chapter 7: Cancel Student Debt?
NO!! Cancel ALL Debt

We hear much of cancellation of student debt. While a worthy effort, not much thought has been given to its implications. And I do not mean economic implications alone. Let us start with a brief examination of a few social implications.

Social Implications

When you give special treatment to any segment of society, you inevitably segment society into pieces - and you automatically sow seeds of destruction. You set one group against another.

No. You should not do that. Are not people whose mortgages are "underwater" deserving of such equitable treatment as cancellation of their debts? One can argue that they are *more* deserving because, while students *knew* they were incurring debt with the accumulation of interest, and compound interest, mortgage holders did not know that "the Market" would cause a collapse of the value of their houses.

"Are you saying that some are "first-class" citizens? Who is to judge?"

No. You cannot be the judge of who is "more" deserving than the other.

Worse. Are you saying that some are "first-class" citizens? Who is to judge?

Political Implications

When you set one group against the other or even more simply temporarily you set one *before* the other, you are destined to fail politically. To win such awesome social and political battles as cancellation of debts on a systematic basis, you need the broadest possible coalition of citizens. To select one group for "preferential treatment" is politically self-defeating.

Theological Implications

Moses and Jesus, as they so evidently did, *invoked* powers of a higher order when they advocated the cancellation of debts. [Yes, Virginia. The Israelites had the wisdom to implement Moses' recommendations, and so did many Kings and Emperors over the years upon installation.] As Transcendentalists, New Agers, and Mystics of all ages and traditions have always known, we have to be in the *same spirit* to win. The program of cancellation of debts has to be our common goal; it has to be a systematic program.

Above all, it has to be designed to benefit the entire population.

Financial Implications

Paolo Uccello, a Florentine painter of the Quattrocento, seems to have been so in love with the newly discovered prospective that he would abandon his conjugal bed in favor of practicing with and proclaiming the beauty of the new tools. Unfortunately, there is no similar anecdote to diffuse the importance of double-entry bookkeeping, an invention by Luca Pacioli, a Tuscan Franciscan, at about the same time. But the science of finance has had, and might still have, deeper implications for humanity than the exploration of the perspective.

"there is no such thing as an externality."

The Beauty, Truth, and Goodness of Double-Entry Bookkeeping. Double-Entry Bookkeeping is a construction of beauty. This is a self-evident characteristic. What is not generally emphasized is that this technique allows us to discover *the truth* about personal, corporate, and governmental affairs. As such it has done and can do *much good* for mankind. But, like any tool, just as it has the potential for good it can also be used to commit much mischief. The biggest mischiefs are those allowed by economists with their fictitious construction of externalities. Mother

Earth suffers most from this lie: If you look at the world as a whole, you discover that there is no such thing as an externality.

Recently, very recently, I made a discovery that might set straight a few millennia of abuse of the lender: The lender, I discovered, is not a hoarder. And then the function of interest, as Keynes intuited, interest as counted in accounting books, became utterly clear: Interest is the reward of not hoarding.

Would the world be better off if people with extra money in their pockets were to hoard their financial assets?

This is a question too deep to explore in these lines. It is the reverse perspective that is of interest at the moment. Much bookkeeping is built on the addition and subtraction of zeros. If you add them - or subtract them - systematically, you do not affect human, substantive relationships one iota. People are just as "rich" as they were before.

If we build on this simple verity, we might avert the impending disaster that is ready to engulf us in a sea of indebtedness. Zeros have been compounded so fast and furiously that we cannot grasp them any longer. If we grasp them by the tail, and systematically reduce them on a recurring cycle every seven years, as Moses advocated and the Israelites were wise enough to put into action, we will all be that much richer together.

If not, we will likely plunge into an abyss with no light in sight.

How Can We See the Light?

Just as recently as the last few days, I believe I have seen a ray of light out of the current morass. With a new twinkle in my eye, I have lately suggested that the Federal Reserve System, and all other Central Banks of the world, can set - anew - our financial fortunes on a steady and just path if they create a new monetary unit for us. Offering a nod of approval to Keynes, I have suggested that our Central Banks ought to create the American Bancor, the Swiss Bancor, the Russian Bancor, the Chinese Bancor.

"Much bookkeeping is built on the addition and subtraction of zeros."

The prerequisite is that the new currency be issued following three rules recommended by Concordian monetary policy. New money should be created as a loan:

> 1. only to create real wealth of tables and chairs, not to purchase financial instruments;
> 2. to individual entrepreneurs, cooperatives, corporations with ESOPs and/or CSOPs in their constitutions, and public agencies with taxing power so that the loan can be repaid;
> 3. at cost.

We thus divert national credit from Wall Street to Main Street.

Toward a World Without Reserve Currencies

If the new money is created on the basis of identical rules all over the world, there will not be any need for reserve currencies. With the help of today's computers, we will know the respective value of each currency at each instant in time. A fundamental condition for mutual respect will thus be established among the nations.

Trade wars? Why trade wars any longer?

Toward a World Without Fear of Crashes

If the flow of new money is directed toward Main Street, let the crash of the financial system come. The sooner the better. No damage will be done to the real economy.

The behemoths of international finance will collapse. They periodically collapse because their design is structurally unsound: Infinite debt does not exist. They should no longer be artificially revived with the taxpayer and bank depositors' money.

"The systematic, periodic cancellation of debts is going to create economic freedom for all on earth"

Few jobs will be lost - at no damage to anyone. Those who want to enjoy retirement, they can; they have accumulated the means to live comfortably. Those who want to start the business of their dreams, they have the knowledge to do so: provided they will create new real wealth, the "new" money will be available to them as well as to any other entrepreneur. Those who might want to remain in the banking business, they only need to inform local banks of their availability.

Economic Implications

What are the economic implications of winning the struggle *for* the systematic, continuous cancellation of debts, as Moses advocated and Jesus in the *Our Father* singled out? The result is going to be as revolutionary as anyone has ever dared to dream. The systematic, periodic cancellation of debts is going to create economic freedom for all on earth; the creation and distribution of money along sacred principles of justice will allow us to create all the real wealth that we individually need.

We shall then no longer be blind followers of the "dismal science"; rather, we will be happily practicing The Economics of Jubilation.

.

Chapter 8: Two Proposals to Stabilize the Monetary System

Abstract

Technically, the first petition proposes that the Federal Reserve System—and other central banks—create a new facility to be called National Credit Notes (NCNs). This facility will issue loans only for the creation of real wealth, such as tables and chairs and professional services; loans at cost; loans to benefit all inhabitants of the land. These are loans, vetted by local banks and issued through local banks, at the request of individual entrepreneurs, co-operatives, corporations with Employee Stock Ownership Plans (ESOPs) in their constitutions, and public institutions with taxing power.

The second petition calls for the introduction of the Mosaic Jubilee Solution into the modern world. Technically, this petition proposes for the International Monetary Fund (IMF) to create an international facility to account for the Systematic Reduction of Debt (SRD). Local central banks are invited to reproduce this facility within national borders to take care of the systematic reduction of debt within each nation.

The purpose of the two proposals is to hopefully avert the next financial crisis and, if the crisis occurs, to be in a position to set things right in relatively short order.

SUMMARY

Two petitions circulating on the Internet are designed to stabilize our monetary system. Their purpose is to hopefully avert the next financial crisis and, if the crisis occurs, to be in a position to set things right in relatively short order. The first petition incorporates the following principles:

The Federal Reserve System (the Fed) in the United States, and any central bank in the world, creates money, not out of thin air as it is commonly believed, but on the basis of our national credit—the credit, the creditworthiness of the people.

The value of the money created by central banks is given by the blood, sweat, and tears of the people of the nation. Therefore, that money, by right, belongs—not to bankers, not to financial speculators—but to the people, as it is recognized by the United States Constitution. Democratic sovereign people of a nation have the right of access to national credit, not as a grant, but as a loan. National credit is a pool of common wealth; it is our common wealth. The integrity of the pool must be re-established by returning to it the money we have borrowed.

After doing its good work, by repaying the loan we destroy the money that was first created. This is an important distinguishing feature that separates this proposal from other similar-looking "money creating" proposals like those of Milton Freedman, Ben Bernanke, or Adair Turner.

The ordered destruction of the money created as loans is one fundamental reason why the call to exercise our right of access to national credit will not create inflation. Another reason flows from the conditions of the loan, conditions that form the suggested new regulatory procedures of the Fed.

By its own will, the Fed can issue: 1. Loans only for the creation of real wealth such as table and chairs and professional services; 2. Loans at cost; 3. Loans to benefit all people of a nation. Hence, loans, vetted by committees of local bankers, can be issued through local banks to individual entrepreneurs, co-operatives, corporations with Employee Stock Ownership Plans (ESOPs) in their constitution, and public institutions with taxing power, so that they can repay the loan.

Just as banks use our credit to give us a loan, so the Fed can use our national credit to issue loans that will be repaid by us, thus making good on our credit/credibility. Unlike other money creating programs, this proposal is distinguished also by the fact that the initiative for the creation of new money in the form of loans resides, not with the Fed or the central bank or the Treasury Department, but with the people. Thus it is very unlikely money creation under the proposed regimen will be influenced by political factors and favoritism and corruption in high places.

The last but not least distinguishing feature is the call for the creation of new money, not on the basis of arbitrary hunches and figures, but in response to real needs, real needs that are expressed as real resources to be energized by the pointed infusion of money into the economy.

A chain reaction of positive events is thus expected to be set in motion: innovation and entrepreneurship will be unleashed; human beings will reach their full potential in freedom and dignity; needs will be satisfied; a fair distribution of income and wealth will ensue; calls for redistribution of wealth will cease; infrastructure will be improved; politicians will no longer be subjected to inherently conflicting demands; citizens will act as sovereigns. Money will get out of politics, because people will get into politics.

The monetary system will be placed on a most stable and just basis: Federal Reserve loans will be issued through local banks, the banks that nearly never failed during recent financial crises. And the world can let the too-big-to-fail operations fail, if they fail, without tearing the national monetary system apart. The taxpayer will no longer be pressed to bear the cost of market failures: no need for bail-outs; no need for bail-ins. Let The Market rule, as it is supposed to do in theory. Let The Government rule over a legal framework designed to foster an economic system that serves men and women, rather than enslaving them.

This proposal results from much history and respects the very dictates of the United States Constitution.

The second petition calls for the introduction of the Mosaic Jubilee Solution into the complexities of the modern world. It calls on the International Monetary Fund, central banks, or newly created institutions to conduct an organized reduction of debt, through destruction of zeros in existing financial accounts.

Debt that benefits both creditors and borrowers is a wondrous thing. Debt that crushes the borrower is a destructive thing that benefits neither the lender nor the borrower. The community, just as the Israelite community of old, ought to be aware of this distinction and act accordingly.

If zeros are systematically destroyed in financial accounts in a way to preserve relative relations among lenders, no harm is done to anyone; indeed, much good is done to everyone.

Strong support for these proposals is expected not only from staunch secularists but also from faithful people of all three monotheistic traditions. They will find here the means for the realization of their deepest aspirations. Members of other religious communities are expected to help unite the world around the programs of action contained in these two petitions.

A. The World of Economics Since 2008

With the welcome addition of billionaires to the chorus, nearly everyone agrees that we are on the verge of a new financial catastrophe. The question that is still open is when, not if. What is the state of preparedness of the economics profession?

The state of preparedness of the economics profession

Unless they are keeping it a secret, or the journals are not publishing it and the press is not reporting it, nothing has changed in academia since 2008. The world of economic theory is still where the renowned Nobel Prize Laureate and New York Times columnist, Paul Krugman, found it in 2014: 'The economics profession has not, to say the least, covered itself in glory these past six years. Hardly any economists predicted the 2008 crisis — and the handful who did tended to be people who also predicted crises that didn't happen. More significant, many and arguably most economists were claiming, right up to the moment of collapse, that nothing like this could even happen." Professor Krugman added: "Furthermore, once crisis struck economists seemed unable to agree on a response. They'd had 75 years since the Great Depression to figure out what to do if something similar happened again, but the profession was utterly divided when the moment of truth arrived."

This is not an idiosyncratic position. More surprisingly perhaps, due to his voluminous investigations, and perhaps just because of them, Thomas Piketty has forcefully made the utter truth explicit: "There is no such thing as an economic science."

What is indeed the status of economic theory? Too many discussions of public affairs are driven by the assumption that grave economic decisions are taken on the basis of sound economic theory—certain, overpowering economic theory, as opposed to pure ideology. This is an assumption as widespread in secular as in religious corridors. It is a fundamental misconception.

A continuing state of crisis

The naked truth is that economic theory has been in a state of crisis ever since the publication of Adam Smith's Wealth of Nations in 1776. What else do major upheavals in the history of economic theory since then signify? Why did we pass from classical economics to neo-classical economics to the marginalist revolution to the economics of Keynes to Keynesian economics to post-Keynesian economics to monetarism to neoneo-classical economics to real business cycle theory to behaviorism—let alone Marxist economics or Austrian economics or Georgist economics or Kelsonian economics; indeed, let alone the splinter programs of research within each major school of economic thought?

These efforts are not accretions to basic scientific knowledge; they are revolutionary attempts to start the economic discourse anew ever and again. They are failed attempts to describe the mechanics of the economic process.

Philip Pilkington has nailed this complex issue down: "Mainstream economics moves forward not through logical development and integration, but through forgetting."

These quotations confirm the validity of steady accusations of irrelevance launched at mainstream economic theory from within and from without the economics profession.

Intellectual irrelevance has not yet translated into political irrelevance. Quite the contrary. If so many economic doctrines come and go, it is because—in accordance with the winds of the moment—they tend to justify the status quo from the right or the left or even the center of the political spectrum. They invariably seem to rationalize the economic behavior and policies of the "powers that be."

We are at a breaking point

But we have now reached a point in which the system is not working for the powers that be either. No one is benefiting from the workings of the system in which we are entrapped. Certainly, the system is not serving the poor; and it has undoubtedly caused a collapse of the middle classes. It is hard to conceive of the case, but we have reached a point at which the rich, perhaps, suffer most from the breakdown of the system—at least from a purely psychological and arithmetical point of view, the rich undoubtedly suffer most.

The rich deserve more attention than they have been given during the last couple of hundred years. As against the general scapegoating of the rich, there is the Biblical assertion that the creators of poverty are, not the rich, but the "wicked." What a politically liberating verity.

From a practical point of view, here is a little parable to unpack. You go to bed with the assurance that your portfolio is worth $3.0 million—not too much money, by today's standards. You wake up in the morning to discover that, because of shenanigans in a far away land, your portfolio is now worth $1.5 million. How will you feel?

And what if, as the rich frequently do, you had borrowed $1.5 million yesterday. That is the condition that pushes some rich through glass windows. Isn't that true?

Wait. Do the poor, do members of the middle class, ever lose $1.5 million overnight? They—we—are blessed with not having that much "capital" to start with. We are not in such danger. Our harts tremble less at gyrations of the Stock Market.

There must be a better way to run the country. And, in fact, there is. But alternative ways to run the country cannot be discovered from within the strictures of mainstream economics. One must abandon that paradigm.

As we have seen above, mainstream economics has repeatedly been proved to be a faulty system by the very academic profession that tries to sustain it. Why wallow in error? Einstein put it straight: To expect different results from repeatedly taking the same steps is not rational; actually, he said, it is "insanity."

The difficulty, of course, resides in choosing the alternative to mainstream economics. The difficulty is that there is a wealth of alternatives, some more serious than others; some better grounded in reality than others; some experientially proven to produce more positive results than others, even though necessarily piecemeal results, for not being thoroughly and consistently applied. And we are all biased toward our own personal preference.

We confuse ourselves and, what is worse, we misdirect our representative politicians by sending them in a hundred different directions. We are clearly at an impasse. To say the least, the impasse is created by analysis paralysis.

How can we ever get out of the current spectrum of opinion?

The most dangerous opinions are these two, and unfortunately they occupy a large sphere of the center of the political spectrum of opinion: Most people are somehow satisfied with the status quo; with much overlap, most other people, while spending huge amounts of energy, seek tiny changes to the system. They do not yet see the wisdom of William Jennings Bryan, whose words resonate even more strongly today: "When we have restored the money of the Constitution, all other necessary reforms will be possible, but until this is done there is no other reform that can be accomplished."

Then, of course, there are the realists who believe it is a waste of time talking truth to power. The subset is composed of people who are afraid of talking truth to power.

A special niche is occupied by the small subset of fanatics who will not lift a finger to avoid the impending disaster because they believe that, amidst the eventual rubble, they stand a better chance to concentrate the people's attention on their pre-selected solution.

Even granted by the relatively few that we must concentrate our efforts on the weaknesses of the monetary system, efforts are still splintered arou this inner circle of ideas: some want "to end" the Federal Reserve System (the Fed), the central bank of e United Sates; many others—intentionally or not—want to subvert its might by creating competitive, local currencies. Two such currencies close to this writer's home are BerckShares and rCredits. There are about 6000 local currencies in the world, at last count. Many want to add one more currency, the one on which they have spent months if not years of effort.

Those who want to "end the Fed" ought to consider what do they want to replace the Fed with. Many of them say: "The Gold Standard." The Gold Standard by itself does not necessarily deny the necessity for a central bank. The major reservations against the gold standard are two: Gold has been and is constantly subject to abrupt changes in valuation; gold is scarce. We need stability in the monetary system; we need sufficiency in the monetary system.

If there are real resources available, if there are real needs to be met, why are resources not utilized? Why are real needs not met? The common explanation is "For lack of money." Well, no. The real explanation is, "For lack of a well-functioning monetary system." The money supply is capable of expanding to meet the availability of real resources. Indeed, in a well-functioning monetary system the money supply is always sufficient to meet the real resources of a country.

Those, on the opposite pole, who want to create a new local currency ought to consider whether any local group has the intellectual and financial resources to create, administer, and safeguard a better physical currency than the state's currency.

And yet, the growing call for the creation of local currencies must be encouraged, not only because of the incomparable ability of local currencies to teach the "nature" of money, but especially because—if and when the financial collapse of state currencies occurs— our lives will rely on barter and local currencies.

What is amiss with all current national monetary systems?

That said, we must be certain about what is amiss with all current national monetary systems. The answer lies, not in the administration of monetary policy, but in the inner conception of monetary policy. The two key questions concern the creation and distribution of the money supply. This is an area in which two diametrically opposed conceptions prevail: one is the European conceptions in which money is assumed to be created and hence to be controlled by bankers; the other is the American conception which assumes that, since the value of money is created by the blood, sweat, and tears of all the people in a nation, the process of creation of money ought to be controlled by the people, and its distribution ought to benefit all the people. New money created on the basis of national credit ought to benefit the common good. New money created by central bankers is not their money; it is our money. Within duly specified conditions, we as sovereign citizens—on a decentralized, democratic basis—have the right of access to national credit and the responsibility to repay the loan.

On this basis, the monetary policy advocated here by Concordian economics, and the fiscal policy advocated elsewhere, does not call for even one cent of redistribution of wealth.

The beginning of wisdom seems to suggest the fastest possible implementation of the following two petitions that are currently circulating on the Internet. They are designed in accordance with the American conception of money—with its deep roots in the Mosaic conception of the Jubilee. They evolve from Concordian economics, whose essential elements have recently been published or republished in the pages of Mother Pelican. The first petition especially is in full accordance with the best thought of John Maynard Keynes, the British economist of world-wide renown who tried in vain to have the idea of a public bank operating in the common interest of the nations implemented at Bretton Woods.

a. A patriotic petition to restructure (procedures) of the Fed

To be delivered to Janet Yellen, Chair, Board of Governors of the Federal Reserve System. In order to function as a public bank, the Fed should

> (1) Issue loans ONLY to create real wealth, such as tables and chairs and professional services;

> (2) Loans at cost;

> (3) Loans to benefit everyone (by funding—through local banks—individual entrepreneurs, cooperatives, ESOPs, and public entities with taxing power, so that loans can be repaid).

PETITION BACKGROUND

The monetary system is broken—the world over.

It is not working for the poor.

It has led to the collapse of the middle class.

It is not working well for the rich, except in an illusory and transitory way.

We have to turn the Fed from serving the few, rather badly, to serving everyone well.

If the proposed structure is in place, let Wall Street tremble or financial behemoths collapse, Main Street will continue to prosper.

To sign this petition, please go to the petition website: http://petitions.moveon.org/sign/a-patriotic-petition-1?source=c.em&r_by=2016207.

In theory and practice, we are so far away from the American conception of money, with its deep roots in the Mosaic conception of the Jubilee, that it is worth spending a few words and dedicating some attention to the topic. In addition to the restitution of the land to the original owner on the 50th year, the year of the Jubilee, Mosaic Law prescribed the cancellation of debts among Jewish people every seven years.

The reasons are many, and all valid. The most important one can be found in the very nature of money: money has real value only at the moment of the exchange; money in my pocket is just paper. If money is concentrated in a few hands, the circulation of money is reduced. When the circulation stops, namely when there is a financial crisis, the value of money is reduced to zero. Chaos ensues. Is not so much more rational to face these issues in a timely fashion in order to avoid certain disaster?

b. The Jubilee Solution: A systematic reduction of zeros To be delivered to Every creditor of the world and Every Government of the world

Reduce all debt to zero in seven years.

Start with a 30% reduction the first year, and reduce all debt by 10% per year every year for seven year(s).

At the end of the seventh year, start the process anew.

THIS PROPOSAL TRULY CALLS FOR A SYSTEMATIC REDUCTION OF ZEROS.

Wealthy people will remain wealthy, as at the beginning of the escalating creation OF ZEROS to their accounts -- because wealth is a RELATIVE thing.

Just be alert: Find ways to isolate the smart ones, who might not join you at first.

PETITION BACKGROUND

The next financial collapse is going to be dreadful. Knowledgeable people are talking of the collapse of $100 trillion. It is the MONETARY system of the world, not the financial system involving a few corporations, which will collapse.

The modern, prevalent solution of letting the taxpayer come in and save the "too big to fail" corporations might not be available at the next meltdown.

Sequestering the deposits of individuals and perhaps even corporations in banking institutions might not be sufficient for the creation of money to run apace with the growth of interest.

General knowledge is gradually growing that charging interest on a loan sets up an impossible race between growth of real wealth and growth of financial wealth.

No matter how much new money is ever created, it is never enough because interest— especially in the form of compound interest—grows inexorably at a faster rate.

Money can never keep up. Interest always wins. But its victory is ephemeral. Bankruptcies result.

Next time around, not even the Fed might have enough latitude to fill the gap.

To sign this petition, please go to the petition website; http://petitions.moveon.org/sign/the-jubilee-solution.

Please, analyze these petitions. If you have questions, feel free to contact me at cgorga@jhu.edu. If you feel you can, please add your signature to them—and ask your friends and relatives to do the same.

To put it very briefly, with the implementation of these petitions, we might avert the impending financial catastrophe that we all know is coming—or at least be in a better position to pick up the pieces afterwards.

B.   (Rationale of Two Petitions)
Curb the "Animal Spirits" of Mankind?

Free capital from the capitalist who is wicked; the wicked are the creators of poverty.

Curb the "animal spirits" of mankind? Spirits that in the short term lead to inflation or deflation and fabulous financial crises in the long run? Is that what we expect of the Fed? Is that the ultimate aim of economic theory? Is that the task of a "civilized" society?

If that is what we want, we fail. And we fail miserably, because we want to change human nature. This is an impossible task; it is not a task for humans.

No sooner was my piece calling for a restructure of Fed's procedures published in the pages of Mother Pelican last month that this realization appeared to me limpidly and forcefully. After many years of working, primarily in economics, I abruptly realized that society is imposing an impossible task upon the Fed, the task of curbing the "animal spirits" of mankind. The existence of this Darwinian conception, of course, has been fully discredited in most disciplines, but it still seems to reign supreme in economics.

As usual in cases like this, as soon as I searched, I found solid evidence to support the validity of not giving such a task to the Fed. A brand new report published last May by the Royal Society for the encouragement of Arts, Manufactures and Commerce, titled Wired for Imprudence, explores six "behavioral hurdles" that make it hard for us to manage money well. The report emphasizes that "Cognitive overload, empathy gaps, optimism and overconfidence, instant gratification, harmful habits, and the influence of social norms can all be problematic for financial capability."

Into this socio-psychological din do we want to throw the Fed? Is that what we really want? If the Fed wages this fight, the Fed is doomed to fail—again and again. There is another way. Concordian economics research suggests that the Fed will have a much better chance of success if it administers national credit on behalf of the nation as a whole. The essence of these recommendations is contained, among other places, in "The World of Economics Since 2008." You can find it at www.pelicanweb.org/solisustv11n09page4.html. They call for the issuance of loans, not grants; loans at cost; and loans for the benefit of all members of society.

You will find there a procedure that would allow the Fed—not to work alone against, as Keynes branded them, the "animal spirits" of people. But to work together with its natural allies. Natural allies are individual entrepreneurs, cooperatives, corporations with

Employee Stock Ownership Plans (ESOPs) in their constitution, government entities with taxing power, and especially local community banks. These entities are all interested, as the Fed constitutionally is, in the stability of the monetary system: steady credit at steady cost. There are many consilient reasons on which to base these recommendations.

The Reason of Customary Praxis

The Fed already works with these entities, but on a last resort basis. It should be the first resort.

The Reason of Order

The rule today seems to be "first come, first served." This is a rule that, engendering fears of scarcity, naturally leads to disorder. The proposed procedures are rules of order.

The Commonwealth Reason

National credit is our common wealth.

The Historical Reason

HEAR YE, HEAR YE

✓ The Massachusetts Bay Colony was the first public organization to issue paper money in the Western world in 1690. In China, paper money was made by the Tang Dynasty in 740 B.C.

✓ Benjamin Franklin explained the rationale for the issuance of paper money in 1729.

✓ As Zarlenga especially emphasizes, the American Revolution was waged to assert this right of the Colonies.

✓ Continentals were issued by the American Revolutionary Government and counterfeited by the British Army.

✓ Lincoln and Kennedy are two American Presidents who made use of this right.

✓ The Populist Movement worked strenuously for a reform of our monetary system.

✓ "Depression Money " was formed as local currencies that kept many communities afloat during the Great Depression.

All this history points to the surging of an innate right to national credit in the spirit of every true American.

The Legal Reason

The proposed recommendations spring directly from the intent of the framers of legislation that established the Fed in 1913. At Paragraph 2, Section 13 of the Federal Reserve Act you find the straightforward injunction that the Fed has to satisfy the financial needs of the nation by "discounting" eligible industrial, commercial, and agricultural paper. There is no eligibility for faltering financial paper there.

How, when, and why the Fed lost its way is a rather well-known story that cannot be recounted here. Here it is only important to realize that in implementing the proposed recommendations the Fed would respect fully the legislative intent of the United States Congress—and might open the road to monetary reform in many other countries of the world as well.

The Constitutional Reason

That legislative intent, in turn, is in full agreement with the Constitutional mandate of Article 1, Section 8, which maintains that, in the United States, the power "To coin Money, regulate the Value thereof, and of foreign Coin" belongs to the people, not the bankers.

The Reason of Unity

If its natural allies are steadily provided with credit, the job of the Fed is done—and done well. A huge sigh of relief will be heard on Main Street. Our communities will be united.

The Political Reason

Our country, and most of the world, is ideologically split as never before. At bottom, the reason is money. It seems that people on the left of the political spectrum want to take money from some people and give it to others. They make an appeal to compassion. The right answers with undeniable issues of justice and efficiency. Neither position is amenable to compromise. And yet, full agreement can be developed on monetary ground. Concordian economics advocates that new money, money created by the Fed be allocated—not as a grant—but as a loan to all qualified "natural allies." National credit is like a lake; it needs to be replenished. Once the issues are thoroughly examined, both the right and the left will agree that this is the right and just way to proceed. Most factions will disappear.

The Neutral(ity) Reason

Money should be created and allocated by the Fed without political interference; this is well-agreed upon in our society. And it is confirmed in Concordian economics. In the proposed restructure of the procedures of the Fed, the call for a loan is initiated at the local level; it is vetted as any other loan by a committee of bankers well-experienced in dealing with fiduciary issues of money. Neither the Fed nor any other government agency has any right to deny or to approve the loan. There is no possibility of "political" influence on the issuance of such loans.

The Economic Freedom Reason

Political democracy is empty without economic democracy. That is why the political class is in such low repute today.

If new money created by the Fed is indeed allocated on the basis of economic meritocracy, a huge step will be taken toward establishing economic democracy in this country, and eventually in the world. Democracy means freedom—freedom for all, not only for the few who know how to play the political game. Make no mistake, no monopolies and no outrageous aggregations of wealth in a few hands would be possible within the sphere of true economic democracy. The ownership of any "natural" monopoly, for instance, will be fully shared among all the participants to their economic success.

The Political Freedom Reason

Do we want political freedom for all? Let us start with the assertion of the right to a fair allocation of the new money created by the Fed. And when that is done, let us have a thorough review of the need for governmental regulations of economic affairs. That is the road we have to travel to regain the political freedom we have lost in this country.

The Sovereignty Reason

Who issues the money is the sovereign.

The Justice Reason

The reason for the existence of so many important and concordant foundations of the proposed recommendations is that their ultimate source is justice. The value of money is created by all the people in a nation—yes, all the people, consumers included. Hence

it is right and just to allocate the new money on the basis of rights rather than privilege. Rights unite; privileges divide.

The Virtue Reason

Only virtuous people can create and keep their money in a virtuous way. In time, the Fed will accommodate the virtues of the right as well as the left of the political spectrum, and thus ease the dangerous political impasse that has lately enveloped our country— and, indeed, the world.

The Practical Reason

Einstein pointed out that it is insanity to pursue the same course of action, again and again—and expect a different result. Whether knowingly or even fully unknowingly, the Fed has tried to curb the "animal spirits" of mankind for over a century now. We have had one worse financial crash after another. Is not time now to change approach?

The Concordian Reason

Chief expected benefit of the proposed recommendations is that the next financial crisis would not threaten the stability of the monetary system, a scary event indeed in a monetary economy. At the same time, the Fed would allow the forces of the market to play themselves out, and thus the Fed would work in accordance with the best available economic theory. No need to curb animal spirits any longer. "Animal spirits" should be left free to roam the country and the world. No one should interfere with the use of PRIVATE money. No one can.

Thus we would move along the road to the creation of a Concordian world in which we do not vainly attempt to curb the animal spirits of mankind. Our purpose is much more modest and achievable: Free capital from the capitalist who is wicked; the wicked are the creators of poverty.

In fact, these recommendations are rooted in Concordian economics, the result of 50 years of research and publication—27 of them assisted by Professor Franco Modigliani, the eminent Nobel laureate in economics at MIT. In addition to the papers published mostly in peer-reviewed journals, a current paper titled "The Concordian Challenge" that summarizes this new paradigm is available upon request.

Needless to say, these recommendations will not be implemented without much discussion and vetting. Your assistance, O Reader, is essential. Many indications also suggest that time is of the essence.

Conclusion

Jesus threw the money changers out of the Temple; and they came back; and they came back. They will stay there until, not Jesus, not any external force, but we the people will throw them out. But how? By exercising our rights, our political and economic rights. Let us exercise our right to national credit; let us take money out of politics through people, informed people, as Dr. Peter Bearse recommends, entering the political process in force.

Afraid of the wrath of old economists and bankers, perhaps, because these recommendation are not coming from their ranks? Be more afraid of the wrecking they are inflicting upon the economic system. Economists know economic theories; they know nothing of the economic process. They believe the economic process is mainly made of money; they do not recognize that even in the sale of a car there are three elements: the car, the money, and the deed of ownership. Bankers, on the other hand, know how banks operate; but they know not the interactive cultural system in which banks operate.

Do not wait for the approval of old economists and bankers. We might wait in vain and until it is too late.

Old economists and bankers are not openly against a Concordian world either. They cannot be. They would not be able to defend their positions. In fact, quite a few economists and bankers who have entered the Concordian world are all for it.

C. Expected Effects of Two Petitions to Improve the Present Monetary System

Two petitions that are now circulating on the Internet are designed to restore the money to the Constitution, meaning that they are designed to reconnect with the best in the American-JudeoChristian tradition, and they are designed to transform the present monetary system in such a way as to assure us all a future that is stable, lasting, and just.

William Jennings Bryan's words are as true today as they were when first uttered more than one hundred years ago: "When we have restored the money of the Constitution, all other necessary reforms will be possible, but until this is done there is no other reform that can be accomplished." The two petitions that are now circulating on the Internet are designed to do just that. They are designed to restore the money to the Constitution, meaning that they are designed to reconnect with the best in the American-ChristianJudeo tradition, and they are designed to transform the present monetary system in such a way as to assure us all a future that is stable, lasting, and just.

The mechanics are as simple as they can possibly be. They are simple, but not simplistic at all. A few of the expected results are given below. A much longer list, affecting many more aspects of our social, political, and cultural life, could easily be provided.

With the first petition, the Federal Reserve System (the Fed), the organization that performs the task of a central bank in the United States, is expected to create money by issuing loans in accordance with these procedural specifications: a. Loans only to create real wealth; b. Loans at cost; c. Loans to benefit all members of society.

The content of the second petition is outlined below.

EXPECTED OVERALL EFFECT

Signing the two petitions and gradually implementing them will cause a deep cultural change: From the worship of power and money, we shall pass to the practice of love and justice. Deep cultural changes are organic; they gradually affect each and every nook and cranny in society; therefore, they are impossible to predict. But here are some of the most likely effects to occur. We shall focus on financial affairs.

On the Meaning of Money

Of course, we cannot even talk of justice in financial affairs unless we truly understand what money is. Technically, money is not wealth; it is a representation of wealth. But this technical definition barely scratches the surface of what money is for us.

Money is so powerful that, to create a new and better world, some want to do away with it altogether. They confuse the thing itself with some of the nefarious uses that are made of it, chief among them is the use of money to control people. This use is not inherent to money but a consequence of the scarcity of money, namely, inherent to the conditions under which money is created and distributed; and these are the conditions that we aim to change with the proposed changes in the procedures of the Fed.

Money, as my barber told me, is the best labor saving device. If you have money, you can pay people to do work for you—and people will find you even if you live in the North Pole. That is indeed important: Money is a store of value. It is this word "value" that gives us an opening into the true meaning and use of money,

Remember when we bought "pet rocks"? We did. And what did we exchange in the purchase of pet rocks? As Rudolph Steiner pointed out, in any exchange we exchange values. We gave our money in exchange for what? Rocks? No, we gave money away, because we loved pet rocks.

Money then is converse a representation of what we love—and not only that. Money is at the same time its converse. Money is a protection against what we fear most.

And what is that? We each have our personal fears, and money unifies us in that as well. Money allows us to purchase economic security. Its loss is what we fear most.

And here the issue gets tricky and technical. As individual persons, we can never purchase economic security. Economic security comes as a result of what we do for our community—and what our community does for us.

Money then is the most syncretic expression of our most varied relationships with other people.

Individually, we cannot either acquire or give economic security—to ourselves or to others. It is only an organized community that can give economic security to individual persons.

On to money in politics, then.

Expected Effects on Politics

Today, money controls politics. No, that is a wrong impression: Money attempts to control politics.

And we attempt to take money out of politics. As Dr. Peter J. Bearse points out, that is an impossible dream. Money will get out of politics only when people get into politics.

Hence, a citizenry always gets the government it deserves. If we think we deserve better than the government we have today, we have to get involved in politics.

To get involved in politics is the same as to learning how to live in concord. There we are then. That is our most difficult task. But if we do not get this goal into our range of expectations, we will never achieve it. Today, this seems to be an impossible task. Too many communities are broken; too many are in a state of war. And money, of course, is the source of much political grief. Love of money is the source of all evil. But there is another way to approach the issues.

Money is a common good. Once we truly understand it, money offers us our best last hope to live in harmonious relationship with each other.

The day in which the Fed transforms the privilege of access to national credit reserved for the few to a right available to citizens, that day many consequences will follow one from each other.

MANY EFFECTS

First of all, that day we will give wings to our entrepreneurship and innovation.

Entrepreneurship and Innovation

Let us free the twin angels of entrepreneurship and innovation and, in a very short time, they will create an amount of new real wealth that will dwarf all the wealth created in the past.

On the Prevention of Accumulation of Wealth into a Few Hands

If new money created by the Fed will be spent only on the creation of new real wealth, many of the existing conditions that favor the Pac-Man Economy will be altered. The Pac-Man economy is that social organization in which money is used to purchase existing corporations, mostly to the detriment of present workers and future owners. If the public money created by the Fed will not be permitted to be used for this purpose, much stability will automatically be added to the economy. The right to the protection of one's wealth will be enhanced. And liberty will be preserved because such operations can still be carried out with private money, but at greater interest costs.

Fair Distribution of Wealth

And the wealth will be fairly distributed, if we tie fresh loans to ESOPs and cooperatives.

The Work of Unions in the Future

What benefit does the worker receive, if the day after the minimum wage is raised by law the market raises the price of goods and services? While people on fixed income suffer immeasurably, room is made only for lower-priced regions and countries to enter the market. Unions, to be effective in the future, will have to learn to tie their dues, no longer to higher wages, but to a fair distribution of the profits—a distribution of equity, a distribution of shares of ownership stock.

And Inflation?

And Inflation? Will not there be inflation with the creation of new money by the Fed? There will not be any inflation with ESOPs and cooperatives in action. Wages are distributed ahead of market decisions; profits are distributed after the market has decided in favor of the product or service being provided.

Besides, under this proposal new money will be created only in correspondence with the creation of new real wealth. The balance between the two will be dynamic and continuous; hence, no inflation will be possible.

Finally, there are substantial differences between the present proposal and similarlooking ones such as the "printing money" of Milton Friedman, Ben Bernanke, Adair Turner, and the adherents to Modern Monetary Theory. These are all varieties of arbitrary grants issued by the monetary authority. The present proposal is based on citizens' rights, it is initiated by citizens, and citizens assume the responsibility to repay the loans. To say the least, this proposal does not carry with it any danger of inflation, because as soon as the loan is repaid, the new money is destroyed. It has been absorbed into the economy.

More Technicalities

Continentals and Greenbacks created in the past as cash were effectively grants that the US Government awarded to itself; interest currently paid on bank reserves are effectively grants awarded to private interests.

Buying and selling bonds from and to the US Treasury and the public, the Fed creates—or destroys—money as debt. Cash on Federal Reserve books is accounted for as debt (borrowed from US Treasury).

The petition calls for the creation of money as an asset: The proposal is for the Fed to create a new facility, if need be, a facility preferably to be named National Credit Notes (NCNs); carrying these notes as assets on its books; these note are to be exchanged at par with existing Federal Reserve notes, in the form of cash (or digits); and creating these notes exclusively as loans, as loans issued at cost, and as loans to benefit all inhabitants of the land.

No More Waste of Technological Innovations

To make our life easier we produce technological innovations. But of what use are they, if their ownership gets concentrated into the hands of existing owners of capital? The majority of us will have to work at two hard-to-get jobs, just to keep pace with the increasing cost of living. The solution to the problem of concentration of wealth into a few hands does not lie in overturning, violently or otherwise, the legal system of the country, but in using the existing laws to benefit the largest number of people possible.

How? It is at this juncture that the future work of unions comes into play: By gradually and legally transforming workers into owners (nmpsey, capitalists), the stage will be set for a broader distribution of the profits of innovation among as large a number of people as possible. Indeed, when more people, through a fair distribution of equity will obtain more income, there will be less need for more jobs. With a less frantic need to create jobs under pressure from nearly all sectors of society, less destruction of scarce resources can be expected—and, indeed, even less damage to the environment.

Also, if the frenzy of the Pac-Man economy is somewhat restrained due to the prohibition to use public money for the purchase of existing physical (and financial) assets, we are going to live a much quieter life.

From a fair distribution of wealth and income, another benefit of inestimable value will ensue: We will need less consumer credit.

Less Consumer Credit

If we earn a living out of our capital and our work, there will less need for consumer credit.

No more work to earn money to repay debts, but work to create the amount of wealth necessary for healthy and "rich" living; no more ecological waste; no more exploitation of human resources. As Emerson realized, from consumers we need to become producers.

The current insatiable need for consumer credit can be abated with a widespread use of Consumer Stock Ownership Plans (CSOPs).

Consumer Stock Ownership Plans (CSOPs)

Consumer Stock Ownership Plans (CSOPs) will be the cherry on top of our future social organization. As pointed out on another occasion, what is never realized in a modern economy is that the poor are an essential component of the economic process. The rich get richer with the increase of production and consumption of the Gross National Product. The rich do not have the numbers to consume the Gross National Product; it is the poor who by their numbers perform this essential function. Should the poor not be compensated for performing this essential function for the rich? Certainly they should. But how? Certainly not with another demeaning hand-out program. Consumer Stock Ownership Plans are perhaps the best possible tools to be used in the near future. The Harvard University Cooperative Store has done this for years. With the development of computers today, it will be an easy taasknto administer such plans. Can you imagine the world in which McDonalds, Stop and Shop, and Macy's at the end of the year distribute a fair portion of their profits among the consumers who have been keeping them alive all year long?

So far we have looked at private personal wealth. By allowing access to national credit to public institutions with taxing power, we will also positively affect our public communal wealth.

Public Money for Public Works

Of what benefit is personal wealth amidst public squalor? Of what benefit is private wealth amidst a crumbling infrastructure of roads and bridges and schools? Certainly, the door to national credit ought to be open to satisfy these needs as well: Public money for public works. Public money for public works should be a refrain to cascade harmoniously from the mouths of economists, financiers, politicians, and administrators of the public treasure.

And We Will Add Fiscal Stability to Cities, Towns, States, and the Nation as a Whole

With public money for public works we will be able to repair our crumbling infrastructure here in the United States of America, still one of the richest countries in the world. We will be able to do that because loans out of our national credit will be issued at cost. Let the private sector get rich in due course, out of executing these public works in the most efficient possible way.

Not only will we be able to refurbish our public infrastructure; not only will we be able to create all the jobs that we need and we want; we will also add fiscal stability to cities, towns, states, and the nation as a whole.

Lest the message be lost, opening the channels of national credit to satisfy personal and public needs is the way to gain a stable monetary system; more than that, that is the way to gain monetary stability for the nation as a whole. The difference is sectoral stability vs. overall stability. Systems cannot be cured part by part; their immune system rejects temporary and partial remedies. Systems have to be cured systematically as a whole complex entity.

THE IMPORT OF THE SECOND PETITION

The attempt to cure the financial system as a whole is the import of the second petition. This petition calls for a systematic reduction of debt through a systematic reduction of zeros. Let us repeat the gist of the issue.

You and Joe have one million dollars each. You are equally rich. Joe's wealth eventually grows by leaps and bounds to 10 million dollars. Clearly, Joe is now ten times as rich as you are. But, by hook and by crook, you raise your financial wealth to 10 million dollars as well. You are now again as rich as Joe.

What has occurred—from a purely financial point of view—between the initial and the final position? Nothing has occurred. There has been only an accumulation of zeros. Hence the second petition on the Internet: To avoid a cataclysmic reduction of financial wealth by financial crisis, the petition calls for an organized voluntary systematic reduction of zeros. This is nothing more than a suggested reproduction of the Mosaic Jubilee Solution.

Financial wealth is a pure accumulation of zeros. This is true for the global economy, not only the American economy.

THE DEEPER MEANING OF THE TWO PETITIONS

The implementation of the proposed petitions to straighten out our monetary system has a deeper intent than just fixing our financial "mess." They go to the core of values of inestimable worth.

Personal Dignity

What do we gain through the implementation of a rational plan of systematic reduction of debt coupled with the gradual transformation of privileges into rights? Apart from all economic and financial benefits, we gain a whole set of values of inestimable worth.

Rather than using power to crush human beings under a mountain of debt, we use rational solutions that turn to mutual benefit.

When we transform the privilege of access to national credit reserved to the few under the current prevailing monetary system into a right belonging to each and everyone of us, we foster the personal dignity of each and every human being.

Personal Economic Security

And personal dignity will be built on economic security for everyone: the poor, the middle classes, and the rich. Even the few will live in a regimen of steady security, rather than under the threat of the pitchforks. No more threats of redistribution of wealth. Thus, there will be certainty of protection of personal wealth for everyone. No more fear of losing one's wealth overnight; no more fear of a financial collapse that will unravel all commercial relationships at once.

Economic Freedom for Individual Human Beings

Economic security built on the basis of the dignity of each and every human being automatically leads to economic freedom for all.

Justice to the Economic System

In turn, economic freedom for all will insure that the social and economic system works with a maximum of social and economic justice for all. We have largely been reduced to a catatonic state in which we do not know any longer what is just; and most certainly we are intimidated from asking that political and economic justice be done to us and to every human being.

Morality to Economics

Thus shall we restore morality to economics: not by preaching; not by practicing methods of moral extortion; but by allowing people to exercise their God-given rights.

Economic Freedom to the Nation

Once we restore morality to economics, we will have automatically assured economic freedom to the nation as a whole. And the chain does not stop there.

Freedom to the Political System

With justice in our social organization, we shall also have freedom in our political system. Money will get out of politics because engaged and knowledgeable people will enter the system in droves. Most of all, we shall abstain from asking our representatives and politicians to play Robin Hood, to steal from the rich to give to the poor. While preserving the right of the rich of access to national credit, we will most assuredly allow the poor and the middle classes to exercise this right as well.

FEAR OF SCARCITY IS THE MOTHER OF ALL EVIL

Fear of scarcity is the mother of all evil. When the Fed creates money, not in relation to gold, not in relation to the hunger of voracious bankers but in relation to the real needs of the country, scarcity will be replaced with sufficiency. And all the potential beneficial uses of money will be unleashed within the nation.

Love and Justice

We do much disservice to ourselves when we forget two essential things: 1. Love is a virtue, a characteristic of our human make-up—just as Justice is a virtue. 2, One cannot be implemented without the other.

Hence, we are going to betray them both when we keep them separated from each other. Indeed, the work has to be extended in the other direction; We must not separate them from all basic virtues such as prudence, justice, temperance, courage, wisdom, science, understanding, hope, faith, and love. Indeed, the practice of all the virtues has to be integrated into one solid unit, in order to become powerful tools of action and thought.

This is the minimum: It takes love to give—and to receive—economic justice.

D. Toward a Systematic Reduction of Debt

Do we prefer a reduction of debt in a systematic, rational, purposeful way?

Or do we prefer to entrust our fortunes to a catastrophic financial collapse of the monetary system?

Today, I would like to focus on two aspects of a petition that is now circulating on the Internet calling for a reduction of debt in a systematic, rational, purposeful way, rather than through a catastrophic financial collapse of the monetary system. This petition calls for the introduction of the Mosaic Jubilee into the modern world.

A Bit on the Rationale

Debt that enriches both creditor and debtor is a blessing. This practice has perhaps been engaged in ever since the dawn of civilization, and it is not going to be extirpated from society any time soon. Nor ought it to be so extirpated. Why? Why should it be?

As soon as debt crushes the productive ability of the debtor, that debt changes its nature from a beneficent to a maleficent reality—and rational people ought to be able to identify that difference and take appropriate action to ameliorate the ensuing harmful conditions from which nobody gains and everyone suffers in one degree or another.

This proposal, which is circulating on the Internet, attempts to adjust the ingenious Mosaic invention of the Jubilee Solution to the complexities of the modern world. The proposal calls for the systematic reduction of zeros in seven years: Start with a 30% reduction the first year, and reduce all debt by 10% per year every year for seven years. The petition goes on to suggest that wealthy people will remain wealthy, as at the beginning of the escalating creation of zeros in their accounts—because wealth is a relative thing. If you and the Joneses have one million dollars each, you are equally rich. Your neighbor's estate grows to 10 million dollars; they are ten times as rich as you are. Yet, once you have increased your wealth to 10 million dollars, you are again just as rich as your neighbor.

The petition recommends further to be alert and find ways to isolate the smart ones, who might not join you at the outsets.

A much longer discussion can be had on the analysis of the economic worthiness of the content of financial estates. For instance, if billions of dollars are evaluated, the difference will be found mainly to reside in bank accounts with more zeros. There was no addition of one chair or one

table or one service in the real economy. There was only an addition of zeros in financial accounts wherever they were held. In a regimen of low interest rates as at present, there is no economic value to those zeros. Even with high interest rates, once the reduction of zeros is systematic, the relative value of any two accounts remains the same.

The Seven Year Solution

Ancient Israel created the institution of the Mosaic Seven Year Jubilee. At the coming of the seventh year, all debt among the Israelites, but not debt involving foreigners, was extinguished. The slate was clean, and business relationships came alive again. It might be wise to use the same structure today, at least until better structures are designed and proven effective. There is nothing to prevent a study of eventual effects that might suggest an improved structure.

A Bit on the Mechanics

It is assumed here that there are many ways to reduce the debt, and if more ideas are proposed and implemented, that would be splendid. I will concentrate on two possibilities, one at the international level, the other at the national level.

Technically, this petition proposes for the International Monetary Fund (IMF), or a new institution created specifically for this purpose, to create an international facility to account for the Systematic Reduction of Debt (SRD) between nations.

Local central banks are invited to replicate this facility within national borders to take care of the systematic reduction of debt within each nation. Whenever the central bank might refuse to perform such function, a new institution—or institutions— could be created specifically for this purpose.

Some Cultural Conditions

Among the cultural conditions necessary to make the present proposal ready for practical application, we need to be concerned with at least two sets of values. The most important is knowledge of all that distinguishes consumer credit from capital credit: In the most stringent expression possible, consumer credit enslaves us, while capital credit has the potential of making us economically and financially free and independent human beings. Hence the recommendations included in the first petition to channel new money on to Main Street.

But there is another no less important set of values implicit in these petitions: To ask for a loan is to make a commitment to repay it; to default is to renege on that commitment.

The converse is less commonly brought forward: To make a loan, to obtain as much return as possible while knowing that the debtor will eventually default because he or she cannot possibly meet that commitment, is fraudulent.

To enter into a creditor/debtor relationship is a two-way responsibility.

Who Are the Potential Supporters of This Proposal?

Many people and many institutions come to mind. Potential supporters are expected to come from Jewish organizations, whether they are public or private, secular or religious. Pride of place is not a silly or boastful position to occupy. The expression "Why didn't I think of it" is a glorious recognition of the exceptionality and necessity of any breakthrough like the design of the Jubilee Solution that offers much to be celebrated. To fully understand the reasons for the development of this idea by the ancient Israelites, rather than Egyptians, or Greeks or Romans, requires an in-depth knowledge of the religious, social, political, and especially international constraints/opportunities of ancient Israel. In addition to the idea of one God, ancient Israelites were the first to come up with the idea of the Jubilee Solution. To this institution, in no small part is due the survival of the Jewish people as a nation, an outward manifestation of a coherent set of shared values, no matter how distant in time or place people happen to be.

The Jewish community may be expected to support this proposal to reduce national and international debt in a systematic, rational way. Yet, Christians of all denominations should not fall that far behind. They are also expected to endorse this proposal for many reasons. Is it not enough for them to do so as reverence for the first public act of Jesus, the expulsion of the money changers from the Temple; his Parable of the Talents, in which hoarding is punished in no uncertain terms; his request of alms for the poor as gifts to himself? Then, even though the unremitting struggle against the ravages of usury was eventually given up as recently as 1971 in the Unites States, this Christian tradition is something to be proud of; it is something that a spark of spirit will revivify in enlightening splendor.

Muslims, of course, are the only religious people who keep the faith against usury alive and well.

It is to be noted that they keep such faith, no matter the practical difficulties and the demeaning snickers from those who know-not. It is equally to be noted that their faith is being rewarded in their creativity in financial affairs. Professor Muhammad Yunus, the creator of modern microfinancing and eventually a Nobel Peace laureate, is by faith a

 Muslim. Those analysts who are fond to point out the minimalist aspects of microfinancing, whether they are Christian or not, ought to remember Jesus singling out the poor woman who gave only two cents to the temple/community—yet, those two cents were all she possessed. The few pennies involved in microfinancing often keep a family alive, productive, and living a dignified life. Is there need to contrast the results of billions of dollars spent in corrupting people and creating too often unnecessary and inefficient public structures?

Conclusion

There is much that needs to be investigated. There is much to refine before these proposals can be implemented. Ideas that fail practical tests are not worth implementing. They sap the energies of people. So, onward with stern criticism; onward with practical or theoretical suggestions to make these germinal ideas come live and bear fruits in the world for many years to come. But enough of analysis/paralysis. Onward with implementation.

Acknowledgments

A heartfelt thank you to all those who have signed either one or both petitions that are highlighted in these pages; thanks to those who will sign them in the future.

Thanks to those who have helped spread the word about the two petitions; thanks to those who are working on spreading the word about the two petitions.

I would like to thank MoveOn.org for playing Internet host to the two petitions.

I would like to thank Mother Pelican, a Journal of Solidarity and Sustainability for playing host to most of the writings that attempt to explain the import of the two petitions and much of the economics that supports them. I am especially indebted to Dr. Luis T. Gutiérrez, its editor, for his infinite patience and readiness to accommodate my last minute pentimenti.

A special gratitude is owned to my collaborators, critics, and editors of many years: David S. Wise, Dr. Peter J. Bearse, and my wife Joan M. Gorga.

Chapter 9: We Must Redirect Our National Credit

We are living under the pall of a bleak future. If we do not change our practices, the future will surely be bleak. Here are two changes to consider.

1. Cancel all debt, systematically, every seven years

Money lent out by the Fed to sustain the market is not productive, therefore the loan cannot be repaid. The web of debt currently created is like a bomb due to explode. The entire system is in danger.

In the past, the rehabilitation of the financial system was achieved with substantial injections of public money through combined efforts of the Congress and the Federal Reserve System (the Fed). This time around such a solution is unlikely to be available. First, Congress is so divided that it might not agree in time on any rescue package. Second, the volume of debt has grown beyond recognition: The combined debt of private and public entities is no longer in the millions but the trillions of dollars. The debt is uncollectable.

If the financial system collapses, credit is no longer available to the real economy. This time around, effects are going to be more deleterious than the hardships imposed by the Great Depression, mainly because most people had a recent relation with the land. Today's generations have to be instructed on how to live off the land. The rational solution, the Jubilee Solution, is to Defuse the Bomb. The rational solution is to legislate a systematic reduction of all debt, not only student debt, down to zero over the course of seven years. And repeat the cycle over and over again. Moses did it. Most Kings and Emperors were able to declare a debt jubilee upon coronation.

Through a systematic reduction of debt, what is being destroyed is not wealth but an accumulation of zeros. Human and economic relationships will remain undisturbed; people will be as rich in relation to each other after as they were before the cancellation of debts. What we have to prevent is the possibility that one individual or one group of people somehow evades the cancellation of zeros. An imbalance will then be created, and some people will automatically and unjustly become richer than the group of people who obeyed the law of the jubilee.

2. Re-orient national credit from Wall Street to Main Street

This is a call that has been frequently and consistently issued by so many sources, the most memorable is the voice of William Jennings Bryan. He was absolutely right. If we do not restore "the money of the Constitution," all our efforts to establish a better society are in vain. Thanks to our beloved Benjamin Franklin, that command is inscribed in the very first Article, Section 8, of our Constitution.

The major reason, we must realize, that this restoration has not occurred yet is that mainstream economics is concerned about inflation and unemployment. There is no common knowledge on how to gain control over the process of creation and distribution of money. Or, looked at the other way around there are way too many suggestions to achieve this aim, from Ending the Fed to the creation of local currencies or to having the Treasury create currency, "spending it into circulation" or giving it out as a grant.

As against such a wealth of ideas, at the core of Concordian economics, there is the consistent recommendation to Mend the Fed—following three procedures. Issuing loans 1. Exclusively for the creation of real wealth, not to purchase financial instruments; 2. For the benefit of all participants in the borrowing enterprise, hence loans have to be issued to individual entrepreneurs, corporations with ESOPs, and public agencies with taxing power so the loan can be repaid; 3. Loans have to be issued at a cost. It would be intolerable if the Fed were to make an exorbitant profit from their operations.

In 2015, I presented a compilation of published papers to the Fed. Jean Durr from the Public Affairs Office of the Fed wrote: "Given your proposal, I suggest that you contact your state and federal representatives."

I wholeheartedly agree with this recommendation. Alone, I have tried and made few inroads. Will people help now that the issue is urgent?

A redirection of national credit

If we follow these recommendations, if we essentially stop "investing" in Wall Street we obtain a redirection of our national credit to Main Street. The trillions of dollars the Fed is lending to Wall Street are going to be burned. By lending them to Main Street these days of Coronavirus, those trillions might also be destroyed, but we are going to save millions of lives and ultimately, we are going to save the real economy at the same time.

Let the behemoths of national and international finance collapse, as pointed out on several occasions, only a few jobs will be lost.

But millions of jobs will be preserved in the real economy. Investment in renewable resources will become possible. A rejuvenation of our social and physical infrastructure will also become a reality.

And what do we ultimately achieve?

A Capitalist Revolution! Yes. What we have today is 1% Capitalism. Through the recommended three changes, we are going to get 100% Capitalism: Capitalism for everyone.

Yet, the term "1% Capitalism" is a misnomer. I woke up this morning with this realization: What we have today is *Socialism for the few; Socialism for the Rich.* Whom is "The State," through the Fed, serving? As pointed out elsewhere, the task of the Fed is not to cub our "animal spirits." If the affluent want to play with their money, they should be free to play. This is true Capitalism. But they are not entitled to ask for the State to bail them out when they lose their shirt. This is True Socialism.

Provided the use of national credit is restricted to Main Street, let the affluent lose their shirt on Wall Street. Let the behemoths of international finance collapse. The real economy will be affected only minimally.

So, truth to tell, what we are advocating is a step toward neither Capitalism nor Socialism, but Concordianism: a world based on the *same* economic rights and responsibilities for everyone, a world of Economic Justice. A Concordian Revolution is waiting to be born. Let us welcome the Concordian Revolution.

Politics will adjust: Let's welcome A Revolution From The Center; A Party—or many Political Parties—of Concord.

Conclusion

What are you waiting for, dear Reader? Get up and grab that prize that you have so long longed for: Economic freedom through economic justice for all.

Certainly, there are a few more things you may want to learn and put into practice. But start with solving the most urgent problems first: cancel all uncollectible debts on a systematic basis every seven years; do ask your Central Bank to adopt the three recommendations of Concordian monetary policy: issue loans only for the creation of real wealth; issue loans for the benefit of every participant in the borrowing enterprise; issue loans at cost.

All the rest will be so much easier to attain.

As it is said in the books of wisdom, a journey of a thousand leagues starts with the first step.

About the Author

Carmine Gorga, a former Fulbright Scholar, is president of The Somist Institute. He is the founder of Concordian economics. He has published eight books and numerous papers, many in peer-reviewed journals. Dr. Gorga is a regular contributor to *Mother Pelican, OpEdNews, TalkMarkets,* and *Econintersect.*
Econintersect is among the Top 100 Sites for Enlightened Economists.

His fundamental book, titled The Economic Process: An Instantaneous Non-Newtonian Picture, has been annotated twice in *Journal of Economic Literature* (JEL). In its -- second -- annotation, December 2017 issue (p. 1642), JEL states: "Expanded third edition presents the transformation of economic theory into Concordian economics, shifting the understanding of the economic system from a mechanical, Newtonian entity to a more dynamic, relational process."

Fifty years in the making, Concordian economics is a new/old paradigm that, in the words of Vincent Ferrini, "has the answers to universal poverty and the anxieties of the affluent."

Reviewing his latest paper titled "Concordian economics - An Integration of Theory, Policy, and Practice," Professor Laurence Katz of Harvard has recently written, "I have read over your paper with interest. You present some intriguing ideas and make the case for Concordian economics. But I must conclude that your engaging paper is not a good fit for the QJE."

Gorga has two petitions on the Internet: One is designed to "Mend the Fed"; the other to "Defuse the Bomb" of the incoming financial crash. He has been described as an economist for the modern world.

During fifty years of research and publication, 27 of them powerfully assisted by Professor Franco Modigliani, a Nobel Laureate in economics at MIT, Dr. Gorga has developed a new system of thought in which everything is logically and technically related to everything else. There are three major component elements to this system: Concordian economics, Somism, and Relationalism.

Concordian economics offers an integration of economic theory, policy, and practice; Somism integrates the Individual in Society; Relationalism presents Rationalism in full bloom, by integrating—through Relational Logic and Relational

Epistemology—the foundational elements of all the sciences into a common mental framework.

From a very practical point of view, all this work accomplishes a single aim: It transforms the "dismal science" of economics into The Economics of Jubilation.

>>>

Gorga holds a Ph.D. in Political Science from the University of Naples and an M.A. in International Relations from the Johns Hopkins School of Advanced International Studies (SAIS). The University of Naples is the University of Thomas Aquinas, Giambattista Vico, Alfonso de Liguori, and Benedetto Croce. His Alma Mater was the first University in Europe to establish a separate chair for economics (separate from the moral sciences).

>>>

He was born in the Deep South of southern Italy, Roccadaspide (SA), in the year of the Lord, as they used to say, 1935, during the dictatorship of Mussolini. That was the midst of the Great Depression, which was soon followed by WW II—and the hoarding of basic foodstuff. The smell of burned flesh is still in his nostrils; and the pains of hunger too widespread to discuss. Clearly, he has deep reasons to be a practicing economist and nonviolent activist

>>>

He is married to the beautiful and extremely analytical Joan M. Gorga; they live in a colonial house at the center of the oldest fishing port in the nation—and the place of birth of the Massachusetts Bay Colony, Gloucester, MA; they have one son, Jonathan, who is a writer and owns the smallest comics bookstore on earth, in New York City, on Carmine Street. Where else?

www.ingramcontent.com/pod-product-compliance
Lightning Source LLC
Chambersburg PA
CBHW040920110726
48006CB00001B/6